Conversations with Angels

Conversations

Edited by Leonard Fox and Donald L. Rose

Translated by David Gladish and Jonathan Rose

with

Angels

What Swedenborg

Heard in Heaven

Chrysalis Books

Imprint of the Swedenborg Foundation

West Chester, Pennsylvania

Chrysalis Books is an imprint of the Swedenborg Foundation, Inc. For more information, contact:

> Chrysalis Books
> Swedenborg Foundation
> 320 N. Church Street
> West Chester, PA 19380

Library of Congress Cataloging-in-Publication Data

Swedenborg, Emanuel, 1688–1772
    [Essays. English. Selections]
    Conversations with angels : what Swedenborg heard in heaven /
edited by Leonard Fox and Donald L. Rose ; translated by David Gladish
and Jonathan Rose.
    p.   cm.
    ISBN 0-87785-177-8
    1. Angels.   2. Private revelations.   3. New Jerusalem Church—Doctrines.
    4. Swedenborg, Emanuel, 1688–1772.   I. Fox, Leonard.   II. Rose, Donald L.
    III. Gladish, David F., 1928–1996.   IV. Rose, Jonathan, 1956–   . V. Title.
    BX8711.A7F6   1996
    289.4—dc20   96—18394
                                         CIP

Edited by Mary Lou Bertucci
Designed by Joanna Hill
Original art by Martha Gyllenhaal, pp. 39, 63, 79, 99, 115, and 129
Cover: Icon of the Old Testament Trinity, c. 1410, by Andrei Rublev. Tretyakov Gallery, Moscow. Reproduced with permission of Art Resource, New York.
Typeset in Minion by Ruttle, Shaw & Wetherill, Inc.

Printed in the United States of America

To David Gladish

Our friend and colleague
who passed into the spiritual world
before seeing this work published

Contents

Preface

BY DONALD L. ROSE

"I have talked to them person to person."

(HEAVEN AND HELL 74)*

How Emanuel Swedenborg treasured the memory of heavenly conversations! He couldn't help being affected by the qualities of the angels as they spoke to him. Writing about one conversation, he exclaims, "I was glad at heart that it was granted to me to speak with angels of such innocence." What he meant by "innocence" we shall see in a moment.

During a conversation with angels, Swedenborg could be walking in a grove or garden in the spiritual world. In *True Christian Religion* 160, he recalls an instance of walking in angelic company: "I talked with them on various subjects, on this among others: That in the world where I am living in the body there are seen at night countless stars, larger and smaller, which are so many suns." These angels, he says, were delighted with this subject and told him that, in their world, angelic communities appear in the distance like stars.

---

*As is customary in Swedenborg studies, the number following a title refers to a paragraph or section number, which is uniform in all editions, rather than to a page number.

At the time of this conversation, Swedenborg and the angels were not walking in heaven, but in the intermediate world where people first come after they have died. It happened that they encountered a dozen people who had recently passed over to the spiritual realm. They interviewed these people and the substance of this interview makes up one of the episodes or adventures that are inserted between the chapters of some of Swedenborg's works.

To find these narratives (and there are dozens of them), a reader has to seek them where they are sprinkled throughout different volumes of Swedenborg's collected works. The idea of bringing them together has led to the compilation of the book you have before you. Most of it consists of stories and conversations within stories, the majority coming from Swedenborg's book on the nature of married love (in different editions titled *Marital Love, Conjugial Love,* or *Love in Marriage),* a work that has proportionately a greater number of angelic narratives than any of Swedenborg's other works. While a substantial number of these stories come from a book about love in marriage, the angels' conversations reported by Swedenborg cover a much wider range of subjects.

Not all of Swedenborg's works contain such explicit episodes of angelic conversations as those related in this book; however, the topic of angels pops up, more or less briefly, as part of Swedenborg's treatment of any number of subjects. Two of Swedenborg's best-known works that do not contain specific angelic narratives are the books popularly titled *Divine Love and*

Wisdom (DLW) and *Divine Providence (DP),* the complete titles of which are *Angelic Wisdom concerning Divine Love and Wisdom* and *Angelic Wisdom concerning Divine Providence.* What is written in their pages has a lot to do with revelations about the actual laws that are behind the events of history and the happenings of our personal lives. In *DP* 70, Swedenborg writes, "The laws of the Divine Providence are arcana heretofore concealed in the wisdom of angels, but now to be revealed so that what belongs to the Lord may be ascribed to Him." In *DLW* 60, Swedenborg brings the wisdom of the angels to bear on the created universe and its wonders. Here he says that, in the spiritual world, he heard conversations addressing both the profound and the minute, about "the wonderful works of God, which are the more wonderful the more interiorly they are examined." At one point in *DLW,* he invites the reader to see the Divine in insignificant creatures of nature:

> Anyone can decide in favor of the Divine on the basis of visible phenomena in nature by looking at [caterpillars]. From the delight of their individual cravings, they strive and long for a changing of their earthly state into a kind of state that parallels the heavenly one. So they crawl into their nooks, put themselves into a womb, so to speak, in order to be reborn. . . . Then, with this transformation completed, endowed with lovely wings according to their species, they fly through the air as though it were their heaven. . . . Can anyone who is deciding in favor of the Divine on the basis of phenomena visible in nature fail to see some image of our own earthly state in them

when they are worms, and an image of our heavenly state in them when they are butterflies?

. . . Can any natural thing have use as a goal, and arrange uses in patterns and forms? Only one who is wise can do this, and only God, whose wisdom is infinite, can organize and form the universe in this way. Who or what else can foresee and provide all the things that serve people for food and clothing? . . . One of earth's miracles is that those insignificant creatures called silkworms dress us in silk and adorn us gloriously—women and men from queens and kings to maids and footmen. And those insignificant creatures called bees provide wax for the lights that add splendor to cathedrals and palaces. These and many other phenomena are visible pledges that the Lord by Himself is controlling through the spiritual world everything that happens in nature.   *(DLW 354; 356)*

The topic of innocence is one that Swedenborg discussed extensively with the angels. In *Heaven and Hell* 276, Swedenborg begins by stating that few people know what innocence really is. "It is indeed visible to the eyes, as seen in the face, speech and movements, particularly of children." In other words, innocence is not just the absence of guilt. There is something present that affects us deeply. There is in innocence a willingness to be led by the Lord, as we are told in *Heaven and Hell* 280. Innocence is by no means something only for children. It is something heavenly stored within us. Swedenborg says that Jesus was talking about this quality when he said that, unless we receive the kingdom of heaven *as a little child* we will not enter therein (Mark 10:15).

A quality that goes hand in hand with innocence is peace. What did the angels say on that subject? Notice in the following direct quotation the way Swedenborg uses the phrase "but the angels said . . ." when they introduce another angle on our earthly perceptions.

> I have spoken with the angels about peace, saying that it is called peace in the world when wars and hostilities cease between kingdoms, and when enmities and discords cease; also that internal peace is believed to consist in rest of mind when cares are removed, especially in tranquility and delight due to success in business. But the angels said that rest of mind and tranquility and delight due to the removal of cares, and success in business appear to be peace, but really are peace only with those who are in heavenly good, for only in that good is peace possible. For peace flows down into the lower faculties producing rest of the inner mind, tranquility of the exterior mind, and joy therefrom. *(Heaven and Hell* 290)

Can the angels share with us something of this peace? Swedenborg learned of angels who provide protection and influence quite beyond our consciousness. Note in the following quotations the emphasis on freedom:

> Their [the angels'] function is to impart charity and faith, to notice the direction in which the person's delights turn, and to modify and bend those delights towards what is good, so far as they can do so in the person's freedom. . . .
>
> The person is in the middle and is not conscious of the evil

or of the good; and being in the middle he is in freedom to turn towards one or towards the other.   *(Arcana Coelestia 5992)**

Let us now consider the angels' perspectives on the seemingly disjointed and haphazard nature of our daily lives. The angels spoke to Swedenborg about a providential pattern. As he states in *Arcana Coelestia* 6486,

> I have listened to angels talking to one another about the Lord's Providence.... They spoke with wisdom, saying that the Lord's Providence is present in the most specific details of all that takes place, though He does not act according to any plan such as man sets before himself, because He both foresees and makes provision for things to come. It is, the angels said, like someone who builds a palace. He first amasses materials of every kind and piles them in heaps, where they lie in no order at all; and what the palace made from them is to be like exists solely in the mind of the architect.

The divine architect of human life is with us from early infancy and throughout our days. Our lack of awareness of all this is like a sleep from which we sometimes awaken as did Jacob when he saw a stairway to heaven. Upon that stairway or ladder, the angels of God were ascending and descending. Jacob said, "Surely the Lord is in this place, and I knew it not.... This is none other than the house of God, and this is the gate of heaven" (Gen. 28).

*Arcana Caelestia, trans. John Elliott (London: Swedenborg Society, 1992). All references to *Arcana Coelestia* in this preface are taken from this translation.

It took a dream to bring Jacob to a new awareness in his life. We spend a good percentage of our lives in sleep; and while we sleep, we dream. If everyone dreams every night, who can tell about the world of dreams? Swedenborg found that the angels could tell him something about dreams. In *Arcana Coelestia* 1979, he states, "I have been allowed very often after dreams to talk to the spirits and angels who had been the source of them." Later in that same work (paragraph 1983), he says that angels involved in our deepest dreams (which we rarely remember) are those who, when they had been people on earth, loved in every way to make other people's lives delightful.

Swedenborg wrote, "It is worth mentioning that when I have woken up and have related what I had seen in a dream, and this has entailed a length of detail, certain angelic spirits would at that point say that such details were in exact agreement with the things which they had been talking about" *(Arcana Coelestia* 1980). He said that the imagery of a dream was actually a pictorial representation corresponding to the thoughts and feelings of angelic beings. A brief way of restating this is to say that many of our dreams are expressions of the conversations of angels.

This work is the culmination of translation by two Swedenborgian scholars, David Gladish and Jonathan Rose. Dave translated all the selections from *Conjugial Love,* while Jonathan provided the selections from *True Christian Religion* and *Apocalypse Revealed.* Each translator also served as the editor of the other's work.

In closing, I'd like to say a few words about David Gladish. Shortly after completing the translations for this book, Dave died unexpectedly of a heart attack. As his son-in-law Ian Woofenden said about him, "Dave was a pioneer in translating Swedenborg. He had a vision of people's being able to read Swedenborg easily and to understand the meaning." All the contributors to this work regret that Dave did not experience the happiness of seeing it in published form. However, as Swedenborg wrote in *Divine Providence*

> Everyone who comes into heaven comes into the greatest joy of his heart.

We know that Dave is now experiencing a happiness that is not ephemeral but eternal.

Bryn Athyn, Pennsylvania
Fall 1996

Conversations
with
*A*ngels

Introduction

BY LEONARD FOX

Although the sacred books of many religious traditions speak of angels appearing to and speaking with people in the natural world, people often react incredulously when they hear that, in the eighteenth century, Emanuel Swedenborg, one of the greatest and most respected scientists of his time, claimed to have frequent conversations with angels. Swedenborg himself realized that most people would not believe him, writing in *Arcana Coelestia* 68,

> I am well aware that many will say that no one can possibly speak with spirits and angels as long as he lives in the body; and many will say that it is all imagination, others that I relate such things in order to gain credence, and others will make other objections. But by all this I am not deterred, for I have seen, I have heard, I have felt.[1]

Swedenborg not only had lengthy conversations with angels, but he underwent what is now referred to as a near-death experience, which he believed to be a special gift from God, so that he could instruct the world on the reality of the afterlife:

> Being permitted to describe in connected order how man passes from the life of the body into the life of eternity, in

order that the way in which he is resuscitated might be known, this has been shown me, not by hearing, but by actual experience.

I was reduced into a state of insensibility as to the bodily senses, thus almost into the state of dying persons, retaining however my interior life unimpaired, attended with the power of thinking, and with sufficient breathing for life, and finally with a tacit breathing, that I might perceive and remember what happens to those who have died and are being resuscitated.   (AC 168–169)

In recent years, reports of experiences of this type have become familiar to us from books, articles, and television programs. In these accounts, the person who has been brought back to the life of this world only had a brief glimpse of the spiritual world. Swedenborg, however, was given the unique opportunity to have his spiritual sight opened so that he could have direct access to both the natural and spiritual worlds at once. He literally spent years being guided by angels and experiencing the sights, sounds, and even odors of heaven, hell, and that intermediate place to which, as he said, everyone must go immediately after death—the world of spirits.

Who was this man, and how did he come to have such remarkable adventures on a plane of existence that remains hidden as long as we live in the physical, material world?

Emanuel Swedenborg was born on January 29, 1688, in Stockholm, Sweden. The family was ennobled after his father, Jesper Swedberg, became bishop of Skara. At the University of

Uppsala, Swedenborg was educated in philosophy, mathematics, and science, as well as in Latin, Greek, and Hebrew.

In 1710, a year after completing his university training, Swedenborg began a period of travel, during which he studied physics, astronomy, and other natural sciences, as well as learning watchmaking, bookbinding, cabinetmaking, engraving, brass instrument making, and lens grinding. Over the next few years, he acquired all the knowledge that the early eighteenth century had to offer in the fields of cosmology, mathematics, anatomy, physiology, politics, economics, metallurgy, mineralogy, geology, mining engineering, and chemistry. He wrote extensively on several of these subjects and was the first person to propound the nebular hypothesis of the solar system *(A Precursory Nebular Hypothesis,* 1734, written twenty years prior to Immanuel Kant's *Allgemeine Naturgeschichte und Theorie des Himmels)*. He made numerous original discoveries in a wide variety of scientific disciplines (such as the functions of the cerebral cortex and the ductless glands, and the respiratory movement of the brain tissues), some of which have been confirmed only in the twentieth century.

Throughout the period of his scientific work, Swedenborg always maintained his interest in spirituality. Indeed, the aim of much of his research in human biology was to find a rational explanation for the operation of the soul, as he stated in the prologue to his 1744 work *The Animal Kingdom.*

During the years 1744 and 1745, Swedenborg experienced a series of visions that had a profound effect on him. Eventually, his spiritual senses were fully opened, and he was able consciously to exist simultaneously in both the natural and the spiritual worlds. He believed that he had been called by God to give a new revelation to humanity; and for the next twenty-seven years, until his death in London at the age of 84, he devoted himself almost exclusively to writing the thirty volumes of theological works which comprise that revelation. In the last month of his life, several of his friends asked Swedenborg to make a final statement regarding the veracity of what he had written. He replied:

> I have written nothing . . . but the truth, as you will have more and more confirmed to you all the days of your life, provided you keep close to the Lord and faithfully serve Him alone by shunning evils as sins against Him and diligently searching His Word, which from beginning to end bears incontestible witness to the truth of the doctrines I have delivered to the world.[2]

Swedenborg wrote in Latin, which was still considered the international language of his time; but, over the last two hundred years, his theological writings have been translated into a variety of languages, and interest in them throughout the world continues to increase.

Swedenborg's experiences in the spiritual world, including his conversations with spirits and angels, are recorded in a number of his theological works. Sometimes these experiences are referred to casually, within the context of the subject under discussion; and sometimes they are deliberately set off from the more abstract theological text and specified as illustrations under the general designation *"memorabilia,"* usually translated as "memorable relations," "memorable occurrences," or "memorable experiences."

In considering the subject of angels and Swedenborg's conversations with them, it is necessary, first of all, to answer the question, "What exactly is the spiritual world?" In his work *Divine Love and Wisdom,* Swedenborg writes:

> The universe in general is divided into two worlds, the spiritual and the natural. In the spiritual world are angels and spirits, in the natural world mortals. In external appearance these two worlds are entirely alike, so alike that they cannot be distinguished; but as to internal appearance they are entirely unlike. The people themselves in the spiritual world, who . . . are called angels and spirits, are spiritual, and, being spiritual, they think spiritually and speak spiritually. But the people of the natural world are natural, and therefore think naturally and speak naturally; and spiritual thought and speech have nothing in common with natural thought and speech. From this it is plain that these two worlds, the spiritual and the natural, are entirely distinct from each other, so that they can in no respect be together. *(DLW* 163)[3]

The external similarity of the spiritual world to the natural one is such that confusion often occurs in the mind of someone who has just died and entered the spiritual world. However, as we are told in *AC* 320–322, the newly arrived spirit will soon experience powers of thought and sensation that far exceed mortal abilities:

> . . . Much experience has shown that when a person comes into the other life he is not aware that he is in that life, but supposes that he is still in this world, and even that he is still in the body.

So much is this the case that when told he is a spirit, wonder and amazement possess him, both because he finds himself exactly like a person, in his senses, desires, and thoughts, and because during his life in this world he had not believed in the existence of the spirit, or, as is the case with some, that the spirit could be what he now finds it to be.

A second general fact is that a spirit enjoys much more excellent sensitive faculties, and far superior powers of thinking and speaking, than when living in the body, so that the two states scarcely admit of comparison, although spirits are not aware of this until gifted with reflection by the Lord. . . .

. . . In the first place spirits have sight, for they live in the light, and good spirits, angelic spirits, and angels, in a light so great that the noonday light of this world can hardly be compared to it. . . . Spirits also have hearing, hearing so exquisite that the hearing of the body cannot be compared to it. For years they have spoken to me almost continually. . . . They have also the sense of smell. . . . They have a most exquisite sense of touch, whence come the pains and torments endured in hell; for all sensations have relation to the touch, of which they are merely diversities and varieties. They have desires and affections to which those they had in the body cannot be compared. . . . Spirits think with much more clearness and distinctness than they had thought during their life in the body. There are more things contained within a single idea of their thought than in a thousand of the ideas they had possessed in this world. They speak together with so much acuteness, subtlety, sagacity, and distinctness, that if a man could perceive anything of it, it would excite his astonishment. In short, they possess everything that people possess, but in a more perfect manner, except the flesh and bones and the attendant imperfections. They acknowledge and perceive that even while they lived in the body it was the spirit that sensated, and that although the faculty of sensation manifested itself in the body, still it was not of the body; and therefore that when the body is cast aside, the sensations are far more exquisite and perfect. Life consists in the exercise of sensation, for without it there is no life, and such as is the faculty of sensation, such is the life, a fact that any one may observe.

One of the basic tenets of Swedenborg's theology is that the visible world—the world of apparent realities that are perceptible to the senses—is a representation of the spiritual. His visionary experiences of the spiritual world may, therefore, be understood on two levels. On one hand, what he describes is, in fact, real: his conversations with spirits and angels took place as he reported them. On the other hand, however, they are symbolic of a higher order of reality that involves immutable spiritual truths that relate to the regeneration—the unceasing spiritual development—of every human being. This can be thought of in the way that the parables of the New Testament are understood. In the parables, people speak and act, but their speech and actions are symbolic of good and evil, truth and falsity, the interior states of heaven and hell that each individual must choose between as the pattern for his or her life. Indeed, the idea that the spiritual world is the cause and the material world the effect appears in practically all of the world's spiritual traditions in one form or another; it is most succinctly expressed by the maxim of the hermetic and alchemical philosophers, "As above, so below." Throughout his theological works, Swedenborg elaborates on this theme, which is central to the entire structure of his metaphysics. Although the two worlds are entirely distinct, there is one level on which there is communication—the level of "correspondences." An understanding of Swedenborg's concept of correspondences is crucial to an understanding of the nature and relationship of the spiritual and the material worlds.

In *Arcana Coelestia* ("heavenly secrets"), Swedenborg explains correspondences as follows:

> Few know what representations and correspondences are, nor can anyone know this unless he knows that there is a spiritual world, and this distinct from the natural world; for there exists a correspondence between spiritual things and natural things, and the things that come forth from spiritual things in natural ones are representations. They are called correspondences because they correspond, and representations because they represent.
>
> That some idea may be formed of representations and correspondences, it is only necessary to reflect on the things of the mind, that is, of the thought and will. These things so beam forth from the face that they are manifest in its expression; especially is this the case with the affections, the more interior of which are seen from and in the eyes. When the things of the face act as a one with those of the mind, they are said to correspond, and are correspondences; and the very expressions of

the face represent, and are representations. The case is similar with all that is expressed by the gestures of the body, and with all the acts produced by the muscles; for it is well known that all these take place according to what the person is thinking and willing. The gestures and actions themselves, which are of the body, represent the things of the mind, and are representations; and in that they are in agreement, they are correspondences.

. . . All natural things represent those which are of the spiritual things to which they correspond. . . .

It has been given me to know from much experience that in the natural world and its three kingdoms there is nothing whatever that does not represent something in the spiritual world, or that has not something there to which it corresponds.   (*AC* 2987-88; 2991–92)

Having established a groundwork by explaining briefly what the spiritual world is, let us now consider what happens to a person immediately after death, when he or she makes the transition from one world to another. In the posthumous work *Five Memorable Relations* (4–6), Swedenborg states:

When a person arrives after death in the spiritual world . . . he seems to himself to be alive as he was in the world, living in a similar house, room, and bedroom, with similar clothes and with similar companions at home. . . . The reason this happens to every person after death is so that death should not seem like death but a continuation of life, and so that the last act of natural life should become the first of spiritual life; and from this he should advance toward his goal, which may be either in heaven or in hell. The reason the recently dead find this like-ness in everything is that their minds remain exactly as they were in the world; and because the mind is not confined to the head but pervades the whole body, it has a similar body, for the body is an organ of the mind and runs without a break from the head. The mind is therefore the person himself, but he is then not a material but a spiritual person; and because after death he is the same person, he is presented in accordance with the concepts in his mind with things similar to those he pos-sessed at home in the world. But this lasts only a few days. . . . When newcomers to the spiritual world are in this first state, angels come to them and bid them welcome.[4]

In other works, Swedenborg elaborates on the reaction of the newly arrived spirit, who is delighted to find that the "new life" very much resembles the old. For example, in his best-known work, *Heaven and Hell,* he writes:

The state of a person's spirit that immediately follows his life in the world being such, he is then recognized by his friends and by those he had known in the world; for this is something that spirits perceive not only from one's face and speech but also from the sphere of his life when they draw near. Whenever any one in the other life thinks about another he brings his face be-fore him in thought, and at the same time many things of his life; and when he does this the other becomes present, as if he had been sent for or called. This is so in the spiritual world be-cause thoughts there are shared, and there is no such space there as in the natural world. So all, as soon as they enter the other life, are recognized by their friends, their relatives, and those in any way known to them; and they talk with one another, and afterward associate in accordance with their friendships in the world. I have often heard that those that have come from the world were rejoiced at seeing their friends again, and that their friends in turn were rejoiced that they had come. Very commonly husband and wife come together and congratulate each other, and continue together, and this for a longer or shorter time according to their delight in living together in the world. *(HH 494)*[5]

This introduction to the spiritual world, or first state, is the one that has been glimpsed by those who have had and reported near-death experiences. But it is only the beginning of a person's journey and is followed by two more states that prepare one for his or her eternal home in heaven or hell. That home is the one in which the person, in terms of his or her spirit, had lived while in the world, although the person was unaware of it. According to Swedenborg's theology, we construct our own interior heaven or hell while on earth and are spiritually conjoined with a "society" in the other world whose members are like our true selves. After death that heaven or hell becomes manifest to the spiritual senses:

Hell and heaven are near to man, yea, in man. Hell is in an evil person, and heaven in a good person. Everyone comes after death into that hell or into that heaven in which he has been while in the world. But the state is then changed; the hell which was not perceived in the world becomes perceptible, and the heaven which was not perceived in the world becomes perceptible.... *(AC* 8918:4)

Essentially, the second and third states constitute a personal and individual "last judgment," but it is not God who judges us; each spirit judges itself as it comes into a profound awareness of its true character or "love"—the love of what is good and of being useful to others, or the love of self and of material things for their own sake. In *Heaven and Hell,* Swedenborg describes the spirit's realization of its true nature:

> When the first state, which is the state of the exteriors, has been passed through, the spirit person is let into the state of his interiors, or into the state of his interior will and its thought, in which he had been in the world when left to himself to think freely and without restraint. Into this state he unconsciously glides, just as when in the world he withdraws the thought nearest to his speech, that is, from which he speaks, towards his interior thought and abides in the latter. Therefore in this state of his interiors the spirit person is in himself and in his very life; for to think freely from his own affection is the very life of man, and is himself.
>
> In this state the spirit thinks from his very will, thus from his very affection, or from his very love; and thought and will then make one, and one in such a manner that he seems scarcely to think but only to will. It is nearly the same when he speaks, yet with the difference that he speaks with a kind of fear that the thoughts of the will may go forth naked, since by his social life in the world this has come to be a part of his will.

All people without exception are let into this state after death, because it is their spirit's own state. The former state is such as the person was in regard to his spirit when in company; and that is not his own state. . . .

When in this second state spirits become visibly just what they had been in themselves while in the world, what they then did and said secretly being now made manifest; for they are now restrained by no outward considerations, and therefore what they have said and done secretly they now say and endeavor to do openly, having no longer any fear of loss of reputation, such as they had in the world. They are also brought into many states of their evils, that what they are may be evident to angels and good spirits. . . .

Everyone goes to his own society in which his spirit had been in the world; for every person, as regards his spirit, is conjoined to some society, either infernal or heavenly, the evil person to an infernal society and the good person to a heavenly society, and to that society he is brought after death. The spirit is led to his society gradually, and at length enters it. When an evil spirit is in the state of his interiors he is turned by degrees toward his own society, and at length, before that state is ended, directly to it; and when that state is ended he himself casts himself into the hell where those are who are like himself.

In this second state the separation of evil spirits from good spirits takes place. For in the first state they are together, since while a spirit is in his exteriors he is as he was in the world, thus the evil with the good and the good with the evil; but it is otherwise when he has been brought into his interiors and left to his own nature or will. The separation of evil spirits from good spirits is effected by various means; in general by their being taken about to those societies with which in their first state they had communication by means of their good thoughts and affections, thus to those societies that they had induced to believe by outward appearances that they were not evil. Usually they are led about through a wide circle, and everywhere what they really are is made manifest to good spirits. At the sight of them the good spirits turn away; and at the same time the evil spirits who are being led about turn their faces away from the good towards that quarter where their infernal society is, into which they are about to come. . . .

The third state of man after death, that is, of his spirit, is a state of instruction. This state is for those who enter heaven and become angels. It is not for those who enter hell, because such are incapable of being taught, and therefore their second state is also their third, ending in this, that they are wholly turned to their own love, thus to that infernal society which is in a like love. When this has been done they will and think from that love and as that love is infernal they will nothing but what is evil and think nothing but what is false; and in such thinking and willing they find their delights, because these belong to their love; and in consequence of this they reject every thing good and true which they had previously adopted as serviceable to their love as means.

Good spirits, on the other hand, are led from the second state into the third, which is the state of their preparation for heaven by means of instruction. For one can be prepared for heaven only by means of knowledge of good and truth, that is, only by means of instruction, since one can know what spiritual good and truth are, and what evil and falsity are, which are their opposites, only by being taught.

(HH 502-504; 507; 510-512)

Before entering the third state, some spirits need to undergo what Swedenborg terms "vastation," which is a kind of purification from spiritual impurities. Every human being has some negative qualities or has become confirmed in some false belief, although he or she, on balance, may have led a good life while in the world. For a spirit to receive divine goodness and truth within himself or herself, and thus in order to acquire an angelic character, these inharmonious factors must be removed. The types of vastations that exist in the spiritual world are many and varied, ranging from mild ones that occur during a state of sleep to severe mental anxiety and pangs of conscience to others that appear to be more physical in nature. Once the state of vastation has been completed, the spirits are ready for instruction by angels:

> Instruction in the heavens differs from instruction on earth in that knowledge is not committed to memory, but to life; for the memory of spirits is in their life, for they receive and imbibe everything that is in harmony with their life, and do not receive, still less imbibe, what is not in harmony with it; for spirits are affections, and are therefore in a human form that is similar to their affections.
>
> Being such they are constantly animated by an affection for truth that looks to the uses of life; for the Lord provides for everyone's loving the uses suited to his genius; and that love is exalted by the hope of becoming an angel. *(HH 517)*

Once a spirit's third state, the state of instruction, has been completed, he or she is ready to join an angelic society, that is, to become an angel. It should now be obvious that, according to Swedenborg, "all angels were born men" *(DLW* 231), so that angels are not spiritual entities created separately from mankind. This doctrine is asserted many times in Swedenborg's works:

> This vast system which is called the universe is a work coherent as a unit from things first to things last, because in creating it God had a single end in view, which was an angelic heaven from the human race; and all things of which the world consists are means to that end. *(TCR* 13)[6]

> In the Christian world it is wholly unknown that heaven and hell are from the human race, for it is believed that in the beginning angels were created and heaven was thus formed; also that the devil or Satan was an angel of light, but having rebelled he was cast down with his crew, and thus hell was formed. The angels never cease to wonder at such a belief in the Christian world, and still more that nothing is really known about heaven. . . .
>
> They wish for this reason that I should declare from their lips that in the entire heaven there is not a single angel who was created such from the beginning, nor in hell any devil who was created an angel of light and cast down; but that all, both in heaven and in hell, are from the human race; in heaven those who lived in the world in heavenly love and belief, in hell those who lived in infernal love and belief. *(HH* 311)

There is a vast number of angelic societies, each one corresponding to a person's "ruling love," the manner in which he or she responds to the divine goodness and truth that constantly flows into the soul and, most importantly, the manner in which that response is transformed into a person's life—in terms of both intention and action.

> A person after death continues to eternity such as his will or ruling love is. . . . The angels declare that the life of the ruling love is never changed in anyone even to eternity, since every one is his love; consequently to change that love in a spirit is to take away or extinguish his life. *(HH* 480)

How do newly qualified angels discover their eternal heavenly home? They are led along paths to various societies, until there is an immediate internal recognition that this is where they belong, where their ruling love is in harmony with the ruling love of others there and where they are recognized by the angels of that society and joyfully received. There is a beautiful passage in Swedenborg's *Divine Providence* about the significance of the paths to the various heavenly societies:

> No one becomes an angel, that is, comes into heaven, unless he carries with him from the world something of the angelic character; and in this there is present a knowledge of the way from walking in it, and a walking in the way through a knowledge of it. Moreover, in the spiritual world there are actually ways which lead to every society of heaven and to every society of hell, and each one, as if from himself, sees his own way. He sees

it because there are ways there, one for every love; and love opens the way, and leads him to his fellows; nor does anyone see other ways than the way of his own love. From this it is clear that angels are nothing but heavenly loves, for otherwise they would not have seen the ways leading to heaven. *(DP 60)*[7]

As Swedenborg emphasizes many times, the spiritual world is, in many apparent respects, like the natural world because all angels were born as human beings. This similarity applies equally to the state of marriage. Those here on earth who have found a married partner with whom they are in complete spiritual, mental, and physical harmony, resulting in true love, are reunited with that partner in heaven, and they continue their marriage throughout eternity. Swedenborg calls this "love truly conjugial"—the term "conjugial" having been used by him to describe this relationship of total union of one man and one woman: "Conjugial love in its essence is nothing else but the wish of two to be one, or, in other words, a will on their part that their two lives become one life" *(CL 215)*.[8] Those who have not been so fortunate during their physical lifetime find an eternal partner in the spiritual world. In Swedenborg's theological writings, there are a great many beautiful teachings on the conjugial relationship and its significance, as a number of the accounts that follow indicate:

> The states produced by [conjugial] love are innocence, peace, tranquillity, inmost friendship, complete trust, a mutual desire

of the mind and heart to do the other every good; also, as a result of all these, bliss, felicity, delight, pleasure, and, owing to an eternal enjoyment of states like this, the happiness of heaven. All of these states are inherent in conjugial love and consequently spring from it, and the reason is that conjugial love originates from the marriage between goodness and truth, and this marriage comes from the Lord. Moreover, it is the nature of love to will to share with another, indeed, to confer joys upon another whom it loves from the heart, and to seek its own joys in return from doing so; and this being the case, infinitely more, therefore, does the divine love in the Lord will to confer joys upon mankind, whom He created to be recipients of both the love and the wisdom emanating from Him.

(CL 180)

... For one who is in love truly conjugial loves what the other thinks and what the other wills; thus he also loves to think as the other does, and he loves to will as the other does; consequently to be united to the other, and to become as one person.

(AC 10169)

Those who are in true conjugial love, after death, when they become angels, return to their early manhood and to youth, the males, however spent with age, becoming young men, and the wives, however spent with age, becoming young women. Each partner returns to the flower and joys of the age when conjugial love begins to exalt the life with new delights. ... I have been told from heaven that such then have the life of love, which cannot otherwise be described than as the life of joy itself. . . . [M]arriages on the earth correspond to marriages in the heavens; and after death people come into the correspondence, that is, comes from natural bodily marriage into spiritual heavenly marriage, which is heaven itself and the joy of heaven.

(AE 1000:4-5)[9]

. . . Love truly conjugial is in its origin pure delight itself of the mind, and that love is the fundamental of all loves. From love is all the beauty of the angels in heaven, for love or the affection of love forms everyone, wherefore every angel is as to his face the image of his love or affection. Hence it is that all the beauty of the angels in heaven is from their conjugial love; for the inmost of their life which shines through is [from that source].

(De Conjugio 2)[10]

We have seen how a person becomes an angel after death, how that spirit chooses his home and a mate. The next question to explore is "What exactly does an angel do?" Swedenborg was granted not only to speak with angels, but actually to see what heaven is really like. For countless centuries and up to the present, oral traditions, books, art, movies, and television programs have speculated on the nature of heaven, sometimes with rather grotesque results. The cartoon image of angels flying around and doing nothing but playing harps to eternity is perhaps an extreme example, but, in general, people have had difficulty defining what it is about heaven that imbues it with "heavenly" happiness. At the beginning of *Conjugial Love,* Swedenborg is present at a gathering in the spiritual world where the question is asked of an angel, "What is heavenly joy?"

> The angel answered, briefly, "It is the pleasure of doing something that is of use to oneself and to others, and the pleasure in being useful takes its essence from love and its expression from wisdom. The pleasure in being useful, springing from love through wisdom, is the life and soul of all heavenly joys." (*CL* 5)

Each individual human being sees and understands goodness and truth in his or her own way and orders his or her life in accordance with that understanding. One person may be drawn more to works—or what Swedenborg terms "uses"—that reflect the virtue of compassion (doctors or nurses, for example); another may want to communicate knowledge for the benefit of those who are ignorant (teachers, for example); still another may have a love of working with his or her hands in order to make life more comfortable for people (a bricklayer, carpenter, plumber, or shoemaker, for example), and so forth. In all instances, the foundation upon which every use must be built is a sincere desire to be of service to our fellow human beings because we love the goodness that is in them, the goodness that they receive from God. Throughout Swedenborg's theological writings, the concept of "use" is given great prominence, and there is a succinct definition given in *CL* 183: "Use is the doing of good from love by means of wisdom; use is good itself." Heaven itself is called a "kingdom of uses," and the heartfelt intention to be useful is a necessary prerequisite to becoming an angel.

> There is no happiness except in an active life. Angelic life con-
> sists in use, and in the goods of charity. . . . [Angels are] images
> of the Lord; thus do they love the neighbor more than them-
> selves; and for this reason heaven is heaven. So that angelic
> happiness is in use, from use, and according to use, that is, it is
> according to the goods of love and of charity.   (*AC* 454)

But what are the uses that angels serve? What do they do throughout eternity? *Heaven and Hell* offers the most complete description imaginable of angelic occupations:

> It is impossible to enumerate the employments in the heavens,
> still less to describe them in detail, but something may be said
> about them in a general way; for they are numberless, and vary
> in accordance with the functions of the societies. Each society
> has its special function, for as societies are distinct in accor-
> dance with goods, so they are distinct in accordance with uses,
> because with all in the heavens goods are goods in act, which
> are uses.   (*HH* 387)

> Some societies are employed in taking care of little children;
> others in teaching and training them as they grow up; others in
> teaching and training in like manner the boys and girls that
> have acquired a good disposition from their education in the
> world, and in consequence have come into heaven. There are

other societies that teach [divine truths], and lead [those who are ignorant of them] into the way to heaven. . . .

There are some societies that . . . attend upon spirits that are in the hells, and restrain them from tormenting each other beyond prescribed limits; and there are some that attend upon those who are being raised from the dead. In general, angels from each society are sent to mortals to watch over them and to lead them away from evil affections and consequent thoughts, and to inspire them with good affections so far as they will receive them in freedom; and by means of these they also direct the deeds or works of people by removing as far as possible evil intentions.

. . . But all these employments of angels are employments of the Lord through the angels, for the angels perform them from the Lord and not from themselves.   *(HH 391)*

Among the uses mentioned in the foregoing passage are those that relate to the care and education of children in heaven. An entire chapter in *Heaven and Hell* discusses this subject, and the reader is referred to that work for details. It is worthwhile, however, reproducing here part of the opening paragraph of that chapter, because it answers unequivocally a question that has been raised in the Christian world over the centuries:

It is a belief of some that only such children as are born within the church go to heaven, and that those born out of the church do not, and for the reason that the children within the church are baptized and by baptism are initiated into faith of the church. . . . Let them know therefore that every child, wherever he is born, whether within the church or outside of it, whether of pious parents or impious, is received when he dies by the Lord and trained up in heaven, and taught in accordance with Divine order, and imbued with affections for what is good, and through these with knowledge of what is true; and afterwards as he is perfected in intelligence and wisdom is introduced into heaven and becomes an angel. Everyone who thinks from reason can be sure that all are born for heaven and no one for hell, and if [an adult] person comes into hell he himself is culpable; but little children cannot be held culpable.   (*HH* 329)

The concept of state is extremely important for an understanding of the spiritual world. Every human being experiences constant variations of state: sometimes we are happy, sometimes sad; sometimes we have feelings of intense love or affection, and sometimes we have feelings of indifference, dislike, or even hatred. Spirits and angels also experience changes of state, although the states of angels do not involve such negative mortal states as hatred in its various forms. Just as our physical existence in the natural world is contingent upon the external factors of time and space, in the spiritual world everything is contingent upon the internal factor of state for each individual spirit and angel.

Angels are not constantly in the same state in respect to love, and in consequence in the same state in respect to wisdom; for all their wisdom is from their love and in accordance with their love. Sometimes they are in a state of intense love, sometimes in a state of love not so intense. The state decreases by degrees from its greatest degree to its least. When in their greatest degree of love they are in the light and warmth of their life, or in a clear and delightful state; but in their least degree they are in shade and cold, or in an obscure and undelightful state. From this last state they return again to the first, and so on, these alternations following one after another with variety. There is a sequence of these states like the varied states of light and shade, or of heat and cold, or like morning, noon, evening, and night, day after day in the world, with unceasing variety throughout the year. There is also a correspondence, morning corresponding to the state of their love in its clearness, noon to the state of their wisdom in its clearness, evening to the state of their wisdom in its obscurity, and night to a state of no love or wisdom. But it must be understood that there is no correspondence of night with the states of life of those in heaven, although there is what corresponds to the dawn that precedes morning; what corresponds to night is with those in hell. . . .

. . . The angels said that there are many reasons [for their changes of states]: first, the delight of life and of heaven, which they have from love and wisdom from the Lord, would gradually lose its value if they were in it continually, as happens with those that are in allurements and pleasures without variety. A second reason is that angels, as well as mortals, have [ego], which is loving self; and all that are in heaven are withheld from [ego], and so far as they are withheld from it by the Lord are in love and wisdom; but so far as they are not withheld they are in the love of self; and because everyone loves what is his own and is drawn by it they have changes of state or successive alternations. A third reason is that they are in this way perfected, for they thus become accustomed to being held in love to the Lord and withheld from love of self; also that by alternations between delight and lack of delight the perception and sense of good becomes more exquisite. The angels added that their changes of state are not caused by the Lord, since . . . [love and wisdom flow in unceasingly from the Lord]; but the cause is in themselves, in that they love what is their own [i.e., their ego], and this continually leads them away. This was illustrated by comparison with the sun of the world, that the cause of the changes of state of heat and cold and of light and shade, year by year and day by day, is not in that sun, since it stands unchanged, but the cause is in the earth.   *(HH* 155; 158)

Time and space do not exist in the spiritual world. There are appearances of these, but in reality, they are changes of state:

> Angels do not know what time is, although with them there is a successive progression of all things, as there is in the world, and this so completely that there is no difference whatever; and the reason is that in heaven instead of years and days there are changes of state.   *(HH* 163)

> Some know that times [in the natural world] in their origin are states, for they know that times are in exact accord with the states of their affections, short to those who are in pleasant and

joyous states, long to those who are in unpleasant and sorrow-
ful states, and various in a state of hope and expectation.

(HH 168:3)

All things in heaven appear, just as in the world, to be in place
and in space, and yet the angels have no notion or idea of place
and space. . . .

All changes of place in the spiritual world are effected by
changes of state of the interiors, which means that change of
place is nothing else than change of state. . . .

. . . Approaches are likenesses of state of the interiors, and
separations are unlikenesses; and for this reason those are near
each other who are in like states, and those are at a distance
who are in unlike states; and spaces in heaven are simply the
external conditions corresponding to the internal states. . . .

Anyone in the spiritual world who intensely desires the
presence of another comes into his presence, for he thereby sees
him in thought, and puts himself in his state; and conversely,
one is separated from another so far as he is averse to him. . . .

Again, when anyone goes from one place to another . . . he
arrives more quickly when he eagerly desires it, and less quickly
when he does not, the way itself being lengthened and short-
ened in accordance with the desire, although it remains the
same. . . . All this again makes clear how distances, and consequently spaces, are wholly in accord with states of the interiors
of the angels. . . .

(HH 191-195)

It is very difficult for us to conceptualize a world in which
time and space do not exist. And yet we all experience, to a certain

degree, states that are superficially similar to those in the spiritual world. When we are asleep, we enter a dream world where we can be transported from one place to another without regard to waking perceptions of space, or where days and weeks can pass in seconds or minutes measured on the clock near our bed. The dream world, as those familiar with the work of C.G. Jung know, is a reflection of our inner states projected onto or represented by external images that are more or less familiar to us.

In dreams, too, we often communicate with others or know what they want to convey to us simply by looking at them, although they are not speaking to us. When we do dream of conversations, the people in our dream almost invariably speak "our" language, regardless of their nationality or the country in which the dream scene occurs (barring exceptional cases where the dreamer is bilingual or has an excellent knowledge of the native language of the country in the dream). Since Swedenborg actually spoke with angels, it is reasonable to question how this exchange was accomplished. In the spiritual world, we are told, there are two kinds of communication—one a sort of telepathy and the other a language:

> Angels talk with each other just as people do in the world. . . .
> Angelic speech, like human speech, is distinguished into words; it is also audibly uttered and heard; for angels, like people, have mouth, tongue, and ears, and an atmosphere in which the sound of their speech is articulated, although it is a spiritual atmosphere adapted to angels, who are spiritual. In their atmosphere angels breathe and utter words by means of their breath, as people do in their atmosphere.

In the entire heaven all have the same language, and they all understand one another, to whatever society, near or remote, they belong. Language there is not learned but is instinctive with everyone, for it flows from their very affection and thought, the tones of their speech corresponding to their affections, and the vocal articulations which are words corresponding to the ideas of thought that spring from the affections; and because of this correspondence the speech itself is spiritual, for it is affection sounding and thought speaking. . . .

The speech of angels is full of wisdom because it proceeds from their interior thoughts, and their interior thought is wisdom, as their interior affection is love, and in their speech their love and wisdom unite. For this reason their speech is so full of wisdom that they can express in a single word what a mortal cannot express in a thousand words; also the ideas of their thought include things that are beyond a mortal's comprehension, and still more his power of expression.

(HH 234-236; 239)

If the essential quality of angelic speech and language is so different from that of mortals, how did Swedenborg communicate with angels? When he was in the visionary state that he calls being "in the spirit," he was able, as he says, to speak and understand the angelic language, as he explains in *HH 255*:

When angels and spirits turn themselves to mortals they do not know otherwise than that the person's language is their own and that they have no other language; and for the reason that they are there in the person's language, and not in their own, which they have forgotten. But as soon as they turn themselves away from the person they are in their own angelic and spiritual language, and know nothing about the person's language. I have had a like experience when in company with angels and in a state like theirs. I then talked with them in their language and knew nothing of my own, having forgotten it; but as soon as I ceased to be present with them I was in my own language.

We have seen that the spiritual world differs in very basic and essential respects from the natural world. One of these relates to the entire concept of reality. In the physical, natural world, we take the reality of what we see for granted. When we look around a room, we see various objects of particular shapes, colors, sizes, and textures. These things constitute our reality. If, however, we were to observe these things under a powerful electron microscope, we would see them in a very different manner; and if, for a moment, our vision were not bound by the limitations of the human eye, we would be totally overwhelmed by what we would experience, and reality would take on an entirely different meaning. Our so-called "objective reality," therefore, is conditioned by our perception. In the spiritual world, however, reality—the *appearance* of things—is a function of internal state: what one sees corresponds to what one is. In *Heaven and Hell,* Swedenborg writes the following:

> The nature of the objects that are visible to angels in heaven cannot be described in a few words. For the most part they are

like things on earth, but in form far more perfect, and in number more abundant. *(HH 171)*

The things that come forth in heaven do not come forth in the
same manner as those on the earth. All things in heaven come
forth from the Lord in correspondence with the interiors of
the angels. For angels have both interiors and exteriors. All
things in their interiors have relation to love and faith, thus to
the will and understanding, since the will and understanding
are their receptacles; while their exteriors correspond to their
interiors. *(HH 173)*

As all things that correspond to interiors also represent them
they are called representatives; and as they differ in each case in
accordance with the state of the interiors they are called "appearances." Nevertheless, the things that appear before the eyes
of angels in heaven and are perceived by their senses appear to
their eyes and senses as fully living as things on earth appear to
man, and even much more clearly, distinctly, and perceptibly.
Appearances from this source in heaven are called real appearances, because they have real existence. *(HH 175)*

These "real appearances" relate, as well, to the paths or "ways" to
heaven and hell that are seen in the spiritual world: they "are real
appearances that correspond to truths or falsities" *(HH 479)*. And
they also apply to the things of angelic existence that correspond
to the things of human life in the natural world. Just as we tend

to think that a person's style of dress or style of furnishings tells us something about the owner's personality, an angel's appearance and that of his or her dwelling correspond to his state of perfection. In *Heaven and Hell*, we learn that angels' "garments correspond to their intelligence" (178), and that "the garments of some blaze as if with flame, and those of others glisten as if with light, because flame corresponds to goodness, and light corresponds to truth from goodness" (179). Concerning their houses, we are told that God bestows a dwelling on each spirit "in accordance with his [state of life, that is, with his] reception of good and truth. [The dwellings] also change a little in accordance with changes of the state of the interiors of the angels" (190).

Finally, Swedenborg's experiences show the foundation upon which the spiritual world is built. The traditions of all the world's religions speak of heaven as being a place of eternal happiness, but Swedenborg's theological writings reveal that the true nature of heaven is a state of joy that results from reciprocating God's love and channeling love and wisdom received from the Divine into service to others:

> . . . The joy the angels have is from love to the Lord and from charity toward the neighbor—that is, when they are in the use of performing the things of love and charity—and in these there is so great a joy and happiness as to be quite inexpressible. This will be hard to those who are in joy only from the love of self and the world, and in no joy from the love of the neighbor except for the sake of self; when yet heaven and the joy of heaven first begin in a person when his regard to self, in the uses which he performs, dies out. (*AC* 5511:2)

The following accounts, all taken from Swedenborg's theological writings and exemplary of his conversations with angels about their nature and existence, illustrate most of what has been written here. We see the surprise and delight of the newly arrived spirit, the confusion and consternation of some when confronted with the errors of their earthly beliefs, the joy of a life with a "soul-mate" and fulfillment of eternal service. The selections are loosely organized to comprise a complete picture of spiritual existence; but, as in any picture, the viewer is encouraged to interpret the content and message as he or she will to find the hidden truths.

It will be difficult for some to accept the fact that Emanuel Swedenborg actually spoke with angels and was given the miraculous opportunity to be an observer of and participant in the life of the spiritual world while he still lived as a human being in the physical world. Swedenborg himself always advised people never to believe something simply because someone said it was so. Rather, he said, it is necessary to use the faculties of spiritual freedom and intellectual rationality with which all people are endowed by God, in order to judge whether what one is told is true. Begin, then, with an open mind. Read these "conversations with angels" and see whether they strike a responsive chord, whether they communicate truths that you have always felt within yourself, but could never express in words. Finally, follow Swedenborg's suggestion:

> Reader, treasure this up within you, and after death, when
> you are living as a spirit, inquire whether this is true, and you
> will see.   (*AE* 984:3)

Notes

1. Emanuel Swedenborg, *Arcana Coelestia,* vol. 1, trans. John Faulkner Potts (New York: Swedenborg Foundation, 1905). *Arcana Coelestia* is a twelve-volume work in the Swedenborg Foundation's standard edition. All further citations from *Arcana Coelestia* are taken from the standard edition and will be cited as *AC* within the text.

2. This statement can be found in the testimony of Benedict Chastanier, published in *Documents concerning the Life and Character of Emanuel Swedenborg,* ed. R. L. Tafel, vol. 2, pt. 1 (London: Swedenborg Society, 1877), doc. 269D, p. 580.

3. Emanuel Swedenborg, *Divine Love and Wisdom,* 2nd ed., trans. John C. Ager (West Chester, PA: Swedenborg Foundation, 1995). All further references to this work will be cited within the text as *DLW.*

4. Emanuel Swedenborg, "Five Memorable Relations," in *Small Theological Works and Letters of Emanuel Swedenborg,* trans. John Elliott (London: Swedenborg Society, 1975). This work also can be found in the Swedenborg Foundation's standard edition of *Posthumous Theological Works,* vol. 1, 2nd ed., trans. John Whitehead (West Chester, PA: 1995).

5. Emanuel Swedenborg, *Heaven and Its Wonders and Hell*, trans. John C. Ager, 2nd ed. (West Chester, PA: Swedenborg Foundation, 1995). All further references to this work will be cited in the text as *HH.*

6. Emanuel Swedenborg, *True Christian Religion,* 2 vols., trans. John C. Ager (New York: Swedenborg Foundation, 1906). All further references to this work will be cited in text as *TCR.*

7. Emanuel Swedenborg, *Sapientia Angelica de Divina Providentia* (Angelic Wisdom concerning the Divine Providence), Latin-English edition, trans. John C. Ager (New York: American Swedenborg Printing and Publishing Society, 1899). This work is generally called *Divine Providence.* All further references to this work will be cited in the text as *DP.*

8. Emanuel Swedenborg, *Married Love,* trans. N. Bruce Rogers (Bryn Athyn, PA: General Church of the New Jerusalem, 1995). This

work is generally called *Conjugial Love.* All further references to this work will be cited in the text as *CL.*

9. Emanuel Swedenborg, *Apocalypse Explained,* vol. 5, trans. John C. Ager, rvd. John W. Whitehead, 2nd ed. (West Chester, PA: Swedenborg Foundation, 1994). In the standard edition, *Apocalypse Explained* is a six-volume set. All further references to any volume of this work will be cited in the text as *AE.*

10. Emanuel Swedenborg, *Marriage (De Conjugio),* in *Miscellaneous Theological Works,* trans. John C. Whitehead, 2nd ed. (West Chester, PA: Swedenborg Foundation, 1996).

I

Setting the
Record Straight

1.

People who have departed from the natural world are asked to form their best conclusions on what makes heavenly happiness.

Once I noticed an angel flying in the eastern sky, holding up to his mouth a trumpet, which he blew toward the north, the west, and the south. His robe fluttered behind him as he went, and it was cinched with a band of rubies and sapphires that seemed to burn and spark. He was flying face-downward, and he calmly glided to earth near me. On landing, he walked around upright on his feet; and then, noticing me, he headed in my direction.

It was a spiritual experience, in which I was standing on a hill toward the south.

When the angel was near enough, I spoke to him and asked, "What's happening now? I've been listening to you blow your trumpet and watching you come down through the air."

"I was sent to summon the most famous scholars, the keenest talents, and wisdom's leading celebrities, from all the surrounding countries of the Christian world," the angel answered, "to meet on this hill where you are and disclose what they thought, understood, and perceived in their heart of hearts about heavenly joy and eternal happiness when they were in the world.

"Here's the reason for my errand. Some newcomers from the world, brought into our community in the eastern part of

*Heaven is such that all
who have lived well, of
whatever religion, have a
place there.*

DIVINE PROVIDENCE 330

heaven, report that not even one person in the whole Christian world knows what heavenly joy and eternal happiness are—and therefore what heaven is!

"My brothers and friends were quite surprised at this and said to me, 'Go down, blow a signal, and gather the wisest in the spirit world where all mortals first gather after leaving the natural world, to report to us based on a number of people's statements whether it is true that Christians have such hazy, dark ignorance about the future life.'"

Then he said, "Wait a while, and you'll see the groups of wise people flocking this way. The Lord will provide a hall for them to meet in."

I waited, and, sure enough, in half an hour I saw two groups from the north, two from the west, and two from the south. As they arrived, the angel with the trumpet ushered them into a hall that was ready, and they took seats assigned to them according to their quarter of the compass. There were six groups or companies. A seventh, that the others could not see for the light, was from the east.

When all were there, the angel explained the reason for the meeting and asked the groups to take turns presenting their wisdom about heavenly joy and eternal happiness. Then each group gathered into a circle and faced one another to review the subject on the basis of ideas they had formed in their previous life, reassess it, and express their considered findings.

After a discussion, the first group—from the north—said, "Heavenly joy and eternal happiness are the same as living in heaven, so everyone who goes to heaven to live participates in its

festivities just the way someone who goes to a wedding participates in the festivities of the wedding. Isn't heaven in plain sight
up above us, and therefore in a place? That's where the blessings
upon blessings are, and pleasures upon pleasures, and nowhere
else! A person is swept into these with full awareness and physical
sensation, thanks to the overflowing joys of the place, when swept
up to heaven. So heavenly happiness, which is eternal, is nothing
but getting into heaven—getting in by divine drace."

Following this statement, the second group from the north
hazarded this conjecture: "Heavenly joy and eternal happiness are
simply the very happy company of angels, and very pleasant conversations with them. This has every face continually blossoming
in smiles and every mouth in the crowd laughing pleasantly at
the wit and banter. What are heavenly joys but things like this in
endless variety?"

The third group—it was the first group of wise people from
the west—offered this after they contemplated their feelings:
"What are heavenly joy and eternal happiness but feasts with
Abraham, Isaac, and Jacob? On their tables will be plenty of delicacies and rich food to eat and lots of fine, expensive wine; and
after the feasts shows and dances by young women and men
moving to rhythmic harmonies and flutes, alternating with the
sweetest songs. And then in the evening there will be stage plays
with actors. And after this, feasts again—every day, to eternity!"

After this statement the fourth group, which was the second
group from the west, presented their opinion saying, "We've been
turning over lots of notions about heavenly joy and eternal happiness, and we've considered the various kinds of joy and have

*The angels that are with
a person do not see his
deeds, but only the
intentions of his mind.*
APOCALYPSE EXPLAINED 185

compared them with each other, and we conclude that heavenly joys are the joys of a nature park. What is heaven but a park stretching from east to west and from north to south, with fruit trees and delightful blossoms in it? The magnificent Tree of Life is among the trees, and the blessed sit around it, enjoying delicately flavored fruits, and are draped in wreaths of the sweetest-smelling flowers. In the perpetual spring air, these fruits form and renew every day in endless variety. What with the continual growth and blossoming of the fruits and the prevailing mild, spring weather, these ever-refreshed souls cannot help breathing new joys in and out every day, which returns them to the flower of youth and with that to the primeval state that Adam and his wife were created into. So they are returned to the garden of Adam and Eve, shifted from earth to heaven."

The fifth group, the first group of intellectuals from the southern quarter, stated, "Heavenly joy and eternal happiness are nothing other than the most power, the richest treasures, and therefore luxuries beyond those of royalty and splendor, beyond that of the nobility. From the people who had acquired these things in the previous world, we can tell that this is what are the joys of heaven and the perpetual enjoyment of them, which is eternal happiness. We can also tell it from the fact that the blessed are to reign with the Lord in heaven and are to be kings and princes, because they are children of the one who is King of Kings and Lord of Lords, and that they are to sit on thrones, and angels are to serve them.

"We know about the magnificence of heaven from the fact that the New Jerusalem, which defines the glories of heaven, will have gates, each of which will be a pearl, and streets of pure gold, and a wall with a foundation of precious stones. So anyone accepted into heaven gets a palace glittering with gold and gems, and each has power, one over another, by status. And since we have found out that joys and deep-down happiness are inherent in things like that and that they are God's unbreakable promise, we can't conjecture any other perfectly happy state of heavenly life."

After this, the sixth group, which was the second from the southern quarter, spoke up and said, "Heavenly joy and its eternal happiness is nothing other than perpetual glorification of God, one eternal religious holiday, and most blessed worship, with songs and jubilation, so it's continually lifting your heart to God in full confidence that He receives your prayers and praises for the divine bounty of these blessings."

Some of this group added that this glorification would include magnificent lighting displays, very fragrant incense, and majestic processions led by a pope with a great big trumpet, greater and lesser bishops and key bearers next, and after them men with palms, and women with golden icons in their hands.

The seventh group, which the rest could not see for the light, were from the eastern part of heaven. They were angels from the same community as the angel with the trumpet. When they had heard in their heaven that not one person in the Christian world knew what heavenly joy and eternal happiness are, they had said to each other, "This can't be true. There can't be such thick darkness and mental dullness among Christians. We should go down, too, and hear if it's the truth. If it is the truth, it's certainly a wonder!"

Every angel is an angel according to usefulness.

CONJUGIAL LOVE 207

These angels said to the angel with the trumpet, "After death, as you know, every person who has longed for heaven and has had some certain idea of the joys there is treated to a fantasy experience of his imagined joys. After finding out what those joys are like—that they are based on groundless concepts and confused fantasies—they are brought out of it and are instructed. This happens in the spirit world to most people who used to think about heaven in their previous life and who have concluded something about the joys there—enough to yearn for them."

When the angel with the trumpet heard this, he said to the six groups of wise people gathered from the Christian world, "Follow me, and I'll lead you to your joys, or heaven."

From *Conjugial Love* 2–4*

---

*These passages form part of a sequence (*Conjugial Love* 2–10) in which an angel allows newly arrived spirits to experience the heaven they envisioned while still alive. These mistaken concepts include thinking of heaven as a continuous banquet (*CL* 5–6; see pp. 107–113 in this volume), as a place of luxury and power (*CL* 7; not included in this volume), as a pleasure garden (*CL* 8; see p. 136), and as uninterrupted glorification of God (*CL* 9; see p. 125). In *CL* 10 (p. 74), the newly arrived spirits learn the truth about the nature of heaven.

2.

Young people, having recently left the natural world, explore a new life.

Once I saw three spirits fresh from the world, wandering around, exploring, and finding things out. They were surprised that they were living as people just as before and that they were seeing the same things as before, because they knew that they had left the former world—the natural world—and that there they had thought people would not come to life until after a final judgment day when they would be endowed with the flesh and bones put away in their graves.

To banish all doubt whether they were real people, therefore, they kept examining and touching themselves and others, handling objects, and assuring themselves in a thousand ways that they were people now, the same as in the previous world. Moreover, they saw each other in a purer light, saw objects with increased clarity, and therefore saw more perfectly.

Then two angelic spirits happened to meet them and stopped and said, "Where did you come from?"

They answered, "We left the world, and we're living in a world again, so we've moved from a world to another world. We were wondering about this just now."

Then the three newcomers began asking the two angelic spirits about heaven. Two of the three were adolescents, and their eyes more or less sparkled with an interest in sex, so the angelic spirits said, "Perhaps you've seen some women."

They answered, "Did we!"

Since they had asked about heaven, the two angels said, "Everything in heaven is beautiful and glorious, and there are things such as the eye has never seen. There are young women and young men, women so beautiful that you could call them the embodiment of beauty, and men so mannerly that you could call them the embodiment of manners. The women's beauty and the men's manners fit together like the pieces in a puzzle."

The two newcomers asked if human bodies were just like those in the natural world.

The answer was "Absolutely the same! Nothing is taken from a man and nothing from a woman. In short, a man is a man, and a woman is a woman in all the perfection of the form in which they are created. Step aside, if you care to, and examine yourself to see if anything is missing and whether you are a man as before."

*Everyone is instructed
after death by angels.*

TRUE CHRISTIAN

RELIGION 255

Again the newcomers said, "In the world we've left, we heard that in heaven they 'are not given in marriage, because they are angels.' So is there sexual love?"

The angelic spirits answered, "Your sexual love, no, but angelic sexual love, which is chaste and without any lewd enticements."

To this the newcomers said, "If there's sexual love without enticements, what sexual love is that?" They groaned to think of such love and said, "How dry heavenly happiness is! What young man could choose heaven? Isn't love like that sterile and lifeless?"

Laughing at this, the angelic spirits came back, "Angelic sexual love, or love as it is in heaven, is quite full of inner pleasures.

It's a very pleasant expansion of the whole mind and therefore of the whole chest, and it's like the play of your heart and lungs inside your chest—play from which comes breath, sound, and speech. This makes intercourse between the sexes, or between young men and women, heavenly sweetness itself, which is pure.

"All newcomers, on rising to heaven, are examined as to their chasteness. They are put into the company of young women of heavenly beauty who can tell what the newcomers' love for their gender is like from their voices, from their speech, from their faces, from their eyes, from their gestures, and from the atmosphere they give off. If it isn't wholesome, the women get away and tell their friends they have seen satyrs or apes. Besides, these newcomers change and look furry to the eyes of angels, with feet like calves or leopards, and they are soon thrown back down to keep them from polluting the air there with their lust."

When the newcomers heard this, they said again, "So there isn't any sexual love in heaven. What is sexual love drained of its vital essence? Aren't these meetings of young men and women dry pleasures? We aren't stocks or stones! We take life in and feel it!"

When the two angelic spirits heard this, they reacted severely, "You don't know what chaste sexual love is at all because you're still promiscuous. It's delight itself in the mind, and therefore in the heart, and not simultaneously in the flesh farther down than the heart. Angelic chastity, which both sexes share, keeps that love from going farther down than the confines of your heart, but there, and from there up, the young man's morality takes pleasure in the young woman's beauty with pleasures of love for the other sex that are too interior and too abundant with happiness to be described in words.

"Angels have this sexual love, though, because they just have married love, and this love is not present at the same time as a promiscuous love for the other sex. True married love is a chaste love and has nothing in common with unchaste love. It's limited to one person of the other sex, without any others, so it's a spiritual love and therefore bodily, not a bodily love and therefore spiritual. That is, it's not a love that invades the spirit."

The two adolescent newcomers were delighted to hear this, and they said, "Then there is sexual love in heaven! What else is the love in marriage?"

But to this the angelic spirits replied, "Think deeper. Consider it, and you'll see that your sexual love is extramarital love, that married love is something else entirely, and that the two are as different as wheat and chaff—or, rather, as man and beast. If you asked women in heaven what extramarital love is, I assure you they would answer, 'What? What did you say? How can something come from your mouth that hurts our ears so much? How can people generate a love that hasn't been created?'

"Then, if you asked them what the real love in marriage is, I know they would answer that it's not a love of sex but love for one person of the other sex, which only emerges when a young man sees the young woman provided by the Lord, and the woman sees the man, and they both feel a married relationship taking fire in their hearts, and he can tell that she's his, and she can tell that he's hers. Love meets love, is recognized, and instantly joins their souls and then their minds, then enters their hearts, and beyond, after the wedding, and in this way makes their love complete—love that grows closer every day until they are no longer two people but, in effect, one person.

"I also know that the women in heaven will swear they know of no other love between the sexes. They'll say, 'How can there be love between the sexes without its being so obvious and so mutual that it pants for an eternal union, for the two to be one flesh?' "

The angelic spirits added, "In heaven they absolutely do not know what promiscuous love is, nor that it exists, nor that it's possible! Unchaste or extramarital love makes an angel's whole body cold, while chaste love or married love makes an angel's whole body warm. Every fiber in the men there goes slack at the sight of a prostitute and taut at the sight of their wives."

Hearing this, the three newcomers asked if there is the same love between married partners in heaven as on earth.

The angelic spirits answered that it is exactly the same. They could tell that the newcomers wanted to know if there are the same physical pleasures there, and they said, "Exactly the same, only much more gratifying, because angelic feeling and touch is much more exquisite than human feeling and touch. And what vitality would that love have without the stratum of potency? Doesn't love vanish and grow cold when this is missing? Isn't this quality the very measure, degree, and basis of that love? Isn't this its foundation, support, and fulfillment? It's a general rule that higher things take form, are established, and stay by virtue of lower ones. So does married love, so there would be no married love without those physical pleasures."

Next the newcomers asked if children are born from those physical pleasures in heaven, and if children are not born, what are the pleasures for?

"Not on a worldly plane," the angelic spirits answered, "but spiritual 'children.'"

All in heaven take joy in sharing their delights and blessings with others.

HEAVEN AND HELL 399

They asked, "What are 'spiritual children?' "

"The physical pleasures join the two partners more fully in a marriage of goodness and truth, and a marriage of goodness and truth is a marriage of love and wisdom. The offspring of that marriage is love and wisdom. The 'husband' in that marriage is wisdom, and the 'wife' is love for wisdom, and both of these are spiritual, so the only offspring that can be conceived and born in it is spiritual offspring. This is why angels don't get depressed after intercourse, as some people in the world do, but happy. They get this ability from a steady inflow of new vigor replacing the old, refreshing and embellishing it. Everyone who comes to heaven returns to the springtime of youth and the potency of that age, and remains like that forever."

The three newcomers, hearing this, said, "Don't we read in the Word that in heaven they are not given in marriage because they are angels?"

The angelic spirits said, "Look up to heaven, and you'll be answered."

"Why look up to heaven?" they asked.

"Because all interpretations of the Word come to us from there. The Word is profoundly spiritual; and because angels are spiritual, they'll give its spiritual meaning."

After a while the sky opened up above their heads, and two angels came into their sight. These angels said, "There are marriages in heaven just as on earth, but only for those who enjoy a marriage of goodness and truth—no one else being an angel. So the Word is referring to spiritual marriages, which are marriages of goodness with truth. You marry goodness with truth in the world, not after death, and therefore not in heaven.

"It says the five foolish women invited to the wedding could not come in, because they didn't have a marriage of goodness and truth. They had no oil but only lamps. Oil stands for goodness, and lamps stand for the truth, and going in to the wedding means going to heaven, where that marriage of goodness and truth is."

The three newcomers were happy to hear this and full of a longing for heaven and the hope of marrying there. They said, "We'll work on morality and the refined life so we can have our wishes."

From Conjugial Love 44

3.

*People recently deceased discuss their visions
of heaven, when an angel suddenly appears.*

Looking into the world of spirits one time, I saw in a field some men dressed in clothes like the clothes of people in the world, so I realized that they had just come from the world. I went closer and stood near them to hear what they were saying to each other.

They were talking about heaven, and one of them who knew something about heaven said, "There are wonderful things there that no one could ever believe without seeing them, such as gardens like Eden, magnificent palaces built by the art of architecture itself, shining like gold and with silver columns in front of them topped by heavenly forms made of precious stones, and also homes made of jasper and sapphire with splendid porches at the front, where the angels go in. And inside the homes are furnishings that neither skill nor words can describe.

"As to the angels themselves, there are angels of both sexes. There are young men and husbands, and there are young women and wives—young women so beautiful that there's no beauty in the world like theirs. But the wives are even more beautiful. They look like the living image of heavenly love, and their husbands look like the image of heavenly wisdom. And they're all young adults. And what's more, they don't know about any sexual love there other than married love. And believe it or not, the husbands have continual potency!"

When the newly arrived spirits heard that there is no sexual love there other than married love and that husbands have continual potency, they laughed among themselves and said, "You're saying incredible things. Such ability is impossible. You must be making this up."

But then suddenly an angel from heaven was standing among them, and he said, "Please listen to me. I'm an angel of heaven, and I've lived with my wife a thousand years now, all of them in the same prime of youth that you see me in now. I get it from married love with my wife, and I can assure you that potency is and has been continual for me. I can tell that you think this is impossible, so I'll discuss the matter reasonably with you by the light of your intellect.

"Little do you know about the primeval state of humans, which you call 'the state of innocence.' In that state all the inner channels of the mind were clear all the way to the Lord, so love and wisdom, or goodness and truth, were married for those people. The goodness related to love and the truth related to wisdom always love each other, so they always seek to unite. When the inner dimensions of the mind are open, this spiritual married love flows through freely with its effort to unite and results in potency.

"Because a person's very soul is involved in the marriage of goodness and truth, the soul participates not only in the continual effort toward this union, but also in a continual effort to bear fruit and produce its likeness. Inward qualities constantly look on an outward effect as their goal, so that they can emerge. When

Angels do not think from things of the body or the world, but from things of heaven.

Arcana Coelestia 6226

marriage of love and wisdom opens the inner dimensions of a person right from the soul, that continual effort of the soul to bear fruit and produce its likeness becomes physical. Because the final effect of the soul in the body in the case of two married partners is in the bodily act of love and since this comes from the soul, it's obvious where this constant ability of theirs comes from.

"They also have constant fertility because from the Lord there radiates everywhere, filling all heaven and all the earth, a sphere of begetting and perpetuating the heavenly qualities of love, the spiritual qualities of wisdom, and, consequently, a worldly manifestation in offspring. This heavenly sphere infills the souls of all people, works down through their minds all the way into the most outward parts of their bodies, and furnishes the reproductive energy. But this can be provided only in people in whom the way is open from the soul, through the higher and lower parts of the mind, into the body, to its most outward parts—which is the case in people who let the Lord restore them to the primeval state of creation.

"I can assert that ability, sexual energy, and manhood have never been missing for a thousand years now, and that I know absolutely nothing about the failure of potency because the pervading sphere I mentioned constantly renews it. It uplifts my spirits and doesn't depress them as in those who suffer its loss.

"Besides, genuine married love is just like the warmth of spring under whose influence everything pants for germination and bearing fruit, and in our heaven there is no other warmth. So for married partners there, this warmth is always present with its vernal influence, and it is from this steady influence that their potency comes.

When we enter a state of love or heavenly affection, we enter an angelic state.

ARCANA COELESTIA 3827

"But reproduction for us in heaven is different than for people on earth. Offspring for us are spiritual—offspring relating to love and wisdom, or to goodness and truth. A wife gets love of wisdom from her husband's wisdom, and a husband gets wisdom from his wife's love of it. In fact, a wife is literally formed into love of her husband's wisdom. This takes place through receiving the output of his soul with joy arising from the fact that she wants to be love of her husband's wisdom. This is how she changes from a woman to a wife and an equal counterpart. It is also how, through the years, love with its deep friendship increases in a wife and wisdom with its happiness increases in a husband—and this to eternity. This is what it's like for angels in heaven."

When the angel had said these things, he looked at the newcomers from the world and said to them, "You realize that you loved your married partners so long as you were erotically excited and that you turned away after gratification. But you don't realize that we in heaven don't love our partners due to erotic excitement, but the excitement comes from love, and that we always have it because we always love our partners. So if you can turn your mind-set the other way up, you can grasp this. Doesn't someone who always loves his partner love her with his whole mind and body? For love directs your whole mind and body toward what it loves; and since this takes place mutually, it joins two in such a way that it makes them just like one."

The angel went on to say, "I'm not going to tell you about married love being implanted in male and female from creation, their inclination toward being legally joined together, nor the male's ability to have offspring, which is the same thing as the ability to increase wisdom from a love of truth. Nor about the fact that a person has real married love and its potency to the extent that he loves wisdom for the love of wisdom, or in other words, loves truth for the sake of good."

The angel stopped talking, and the newcomers began to realize from the tone of his voice that there can be continual potency. This raised their spirits, so they said, "Oh, how lucky the angels are! We can tell that you people in heaven stay in the condition of young adults forever, so you always have the potency of that age. But tell us how we could get this potency too!"

The angel answered, "Avoid adulteries as hellish, come to the Lord, and you'll have it."

They said, "We'll avoid them as hellish, and we'll go to the Lord."

But the angel responded, "You can't avoid adulteries as hellish evils unless you avoid other evils in the same way, because adulteries are a composite of them all. And unless you avoid them you can't come to the Lord. The Lord doesn't accept them."

Then the angel left, and the new spirits went away disappointed.

From *Conjugial Love* 355–356

4.

An evil spirit, arising from hell, proudly shows off his "superior" learning.

One time an evil spirit came up from hell by permission. He had a woman with him. He came up to the house where I was. When I saw them I closed the window, but I still talked to them through the glass. I asked the evil spirit where he came from. He said from a consortium of his colleagues. I asked where the woman was from, and he said the same thing. She belonged to a gang of sirens. These sirens are skilled at using fantasies to present themselves with all different kinds of clothing, physique, and accessories. First they'll give themselves the body of Venus, then ancient Greek makeup, then deck themselves out with the garlands and Greek capes of a queen, and strut magnificently, swinging a silver cane. That's what concubines are like in the world of spirits, and they work hard at creating these fantasies. (A fantasy is created by means of a sensual thought when the thought images from any deeper levels are closed off.)

I asked the evil spirit whether she was his wife. He replied, "What's a wife? I don't know what that is. Nobody in my community knows what that is. She is my concubine." And then she aroused the lust in him, which is another thing sirens are very good at. And so he kissed her and said, "Ah, my female Adonis!"

No angels or spirits were created as such, but were born as people first.

DIVINE PROVIDENCE 220

But on to something more serious. I asked the evil spirit what he did for a living. And he said, "Oh, I'm a scholar! Don't you see the laurel wreath on my head?" His "Adonis" used her skill to blow this into existence, and she put it on him from behind. And I said, "Since you come from a community where there are teachers, tell me what you believe and what your colleagues believe about God." He replied, "Our God is the universe, which we also call nature. The simple among us call it the atmosphere, which to them means the air, while the wise also call it the atmosphere, but they include outer space. God, heaven, angels, and the like—the subjects of many people's many fables in this world—are empty words and illusions caused by the strange phenomena in the sky that play before the eyes of many people here. Isn't everything that appears on the earth created by the sun? Isn't it from the sun's return every spring that insects are born, both the winged and the flightless? And isn't it the sun's heat that causes birds to love each other mutually and reproduce? And isn't it when the land has been warmed by the sun that it turns seeds into shoots, and eventually into fruit as its offspring? Isn't it obvious then that the universe is god, and nature is the goddess who, as spouse of the universe, conceives, gives birth to, raises, and nurtures those seeds?"

Then I asked him what his community, and what he himself, believes about religion. He answered, "To those of us more learned than the common herd, religion is nothing more than a toy for the lower class to play with. It is like a gentle wind around what their minds sense and imagine, and in that wind fly mental pictures of piety like butterflies in the air. And their belief, which connects those pious pictures into a kind of chain, is like a caterpillar in a cocoon, then flying out as the king of butterflies. Those in the brotherhood of the unschooled love imaginings from beyond the senses of the body and its thoughts, since they long to fly. So they even go so far as to make wings for themselves and show themselves off before earth-dwellers, in order to say, 'Look at me!' But *we* believe what we have seen, and we love what we are touching." And at that point he touched his concubine and said, "This I believe in, because I see it and I touch it. But those other delusions we throw out of our windows overlooking the street, and drive them away with a blast of laughter."

Afterwards I asked what he and his colleagues think about heaven and hell. He laughed too loud and replied, "What is heaven except the ethereal firmament at its highest point? And what are the angels there except spots wandering around the sun? And what are archangels except comets with a long tail where the whole gang of them live? And what else is hell except the swamplands where the frogs and crocodiles turn into devils in your imagination? Anything beyond these visions of heaven and hell is nonsense made up by someone high up in the clergy to win glory from the ignorant population."

But he said all these things exactly as he had thought of them in the world, not realizing that he was living after death, and forgetting everything he had heard when he first entered the world of spirits. So even when questioned about life after death, he retorted, "It is a figment of the imagination. Perhaps some outpouring arising from a cadaver in a tomb but looking human, or else what they call ghosts, which some tell stories about, has introduced such an idea into mankind's fantasies."

People are in equilibrium. They are in freedom to accept good and its truth from heaven or evil and its falsity from hell.

HEAVEN AND HELL 537

On hearing this I could no longer keep myself from bursting out laughing. And I said, "Evil spirit, you're too crazy to be insane! What are you now? Aren't you human in form? Don't you see and speak and hear and walk? Recall, if you will, that you once lived in another world which you have forgotten, and now you are living after death, and you said just what you used to say." And the power of recollection was granted to him, and he did remember. He felt ashamed, and exclaimed, "I am insane! I remember now seeing heaven up above, and there I heard angels telling things beyond words. But that was all shortly after I arrived here. Now I'll hold on to this and tell it to the colleagues of mine I left back home. And maybe then they'll feel ashamed as I did!" And he kept it in his mouth that he would call them insane, but as he went back down oblivion drove the memory away, and when he was there he was as insane as they were, and called what he had heard from me insanities.

From *True Christian Religion* 80

II

Finding Your Path

Newly arrived spirits find their way to their heavenly home.

Preparation for heaven takes place in the so-called world of spirits, which is midway between heaven and hell. All who have been
prepared for heaven, after their time has been completed, develop
an intense desire to go there. So their eyes are opened, and they
see a path that leads in the direction of some community in
heaven. They take this path and head up it. At the top there is a
gateway with a gatekeeper. He opens the gate and they walk in
right away. Then the person in charge of the community sends an
investigator to meet them, who conveys the message that they
should go farther into the community and find out whether there
is a house anywhere that they recognize as their own, for there is
a brand new house for every newly arrived angel. And if they find
one, they send back a message to that effect and stay there. But if
they don't find one, they return and say that they didn't see one.
And then some wise person explores them to see if their light
agrees with the light in that community, and even more so, their
heat. For at its essence the light of heaven is divine truth and its
heat is divine goodness. Both stream down from the Lord as the
sun there. If they have a different light and heat (meaning a different truth and goodness) from the light and heat of that community, they are not accepted.

*Angels from the Lord
lead and protect us every
moment and every
moment of every
moment.*

Arcana Coelestia 5992

So they leave there and wander the pathways opened up from one community to another until they find one that is in complete agreement with what they love and care for. And that becomes their home forever, because they are among their own kind, just as if they were among friends and relatives whom they love because they share a fondness for the same sort of things. And there they are in the bliss of their life and in their heart's delight from a sense of peace in their souls. For in the light and heat of heaven, there is an inexpressible delight that everyone shares with everyone else. This is what happens with those who become angels.

Now those who are into doing evil and lying, too, are allowed with permission to go up to heaven. But when they get there, they start to have difficulty breathing. Soon their vision blurs, their intellect becomes dark, their thought process shuts down, the glazed look of death comes over their eyes, and they stand there like lifeless lumps. Then they start to feel heart palpitations, constriction in their chest, overwhelming mental distress, and a greater and greater sense of torture. By this point, they are twisting and thrashing like a snake by the fire. So they roll away and throw themselves off a cliff that appears to them. They don't rest until they are in hell with their own kind, where they can breathe and where their heart is free to beat. After that they hate heaven and reject the truth and blaspheme the Lord at heart, thinking that the torture and torment they experienced in heaven was His doing.

From this information alone you can see what kind of final outcome awaits those who see no value in what is true, even though it makes the light in which the angels of heaven live, and no value in what is good, even though it makes the heat in which the angels of heaven live. You can also see how wrong it is to be-lieve that just being let into heaven would enable you to enjoy heavenly bliss. For nowadays people believe that to get into heaven all you need is the Lord's mercy and that getting into heaven is like our coming into a house where there's a wedding, and at the same time coming into the joy and happiness that are there. But people need to know that in the spiritual world feelings are communal rather than individual, since people are spirits at that point and feelings constitute a spirit's life. Their thoughts originate in and are driven by their feelings. Similar feelings bring spirits together, while opposite ones drive them apart; and a feel-ing opposite to their own is a form of torture for them. So a devil feels tortured in heaven; an angel feels tortured in hell. For this reason all spirits have to be grouped accurately according to the diversity, variety, and differences of their feelings stemming from their overall state of love.

From Apocalypse Revealed 611

6.

A newcomer in the spiritual world learns what happiness is.

I once spoke with a newly arrived spirit who had thought about heaven and hell a lot when he was in the world. The term "newly arrived spirits" refers to people recently deceased, who are called spirits because they are then spiritual people.

As this person entered spiritual life, he began to think about heaven and hell, as usual, and he found himself happy when thinking about heaven and depressed when thinking about hell. When he realized he was in the spiritual world, he kept asking where heaven and hell are, and what each place is and what it is like.

People had told him, "Heaven's above your head, and hell's below your feet, because you're in the world of spirits now, which is halfway between heaven and hell. But what heaven and hell are we can't explain in a few words."

Then, because he had a burning desire to know, he fell to his knees and prayed devoutly to the Lord to be instructed; and at his right hand there appeared an angel! The angel helped him up and said, "You've prayed to be instructed about heaven and hell. Ask around and find out what happiness is, and you'll know." Having said this, the angel disappeared.

Then the new spirit said to himself, "What is this? 'Ask around and find out what happiness is, and you'll know what heaven and hell are and what they're like?'"

He left that place, and as he wandered here and there, he asked people he met, "Please say what happiness is, if you don't mind."

Some said, "What kind of question is that? Who doesn't know what happiness is? Isn't it joy and gladness? So happiness is happiness, one way or another. We can't see any difference."

Others said, "Happiness is a light heart, because when your heart is light your face is cheerful, your speech is witty, you act playful, and you feel good all over."

Still others said, "Happiness is just to feast, eat fine food, drink and get tipsy on noble wine, and then chat about different things—especially the diversions of love and sex."

Hearing all this the disappointed new spirit said to himself, "These answers are crude and uncouth. Those pleasures are neither heaven nor hell. I wish I'd meet some wise people."

And he left them and asked, "Where are some wise people?"

And then he was observed by a certain angelic spirit, who said, "I notice that you're burning with a desire to know what's broadly characteristic of heaven and broadly characteristic of hell. It's happiness, so I'll take you up onto a hill where, each day, people gather who analyze results, and people who look into the causes, and people who explore the reasons—three groups. The ones who inspect results are called spirits of facts, or abstractly, the Facts. Those who look into the causes are called spirits of information, or abstractly, the Information. Those who explore the reasons are called spirits of wisdom, or abstractly, Wisdom. Just above these people, in heaven, are angels who view the causes in light of the reasons and the results in light of the causes. From these angels the three groups have enlightenment."

Angels in heaven take joy in sharing their delight and blessings with others.

HEAVEN AND HELL 399

Then, taking the spirit by the hand, he led him up onto the hill to the group made up of those who explore the reasons and are called Wisdom.

The newcomer said to them, "Excuse my coming up to you. It's because from childhood I've thought about heaven and hell, and I've just arrived in this world; and when I did, some people I met said that heaven is above my head and hell is below my feet here. But they didn't say what heaven and hell are and what they're like. Due to thinking about heaven and hell all the time, I was desperate; so I prayed too, and an angel was there and said, 'Ask around and find out what happiness is, and you'll know.'

"I've asked, but uselessly so far. So, if you will, please teach me what happiness is."

The wise people answered, "Happiness is all that everyone in heaven lives for and all that everyone in hell lives for. For those in heaven, happiness has to do with what is good and true; but for those in hell, happiness has to do with what is evil and untrue because all happiness relates to love, and love is the essence of a person's life. So just as a person is a person according to his kind of love, he's a person according to his kind of happiness.

"Love in action gives a feeling of happiness. In heaven it acts with wisdom; in hell it acts with folly. Either way it makes its subject happy.

"But heaven and hell have opposite pleasures because they have opposite loves. Heaven has the love of being helpful and the happiness this gives; hell has the love of being harmful and the happiness this gives. So if you know what happiness is, you do know what heaven and hell are and what they're like.

"But ask around some more and find out what happiness is from the people who look into the causes and are called the Information. They're to the right from here."

The newcomer left, went to the Information, told them why he had come, and asked them to teach him what happiness is.

Happy to be asked, they said, "It's true that whoever recognizes happiness realizes what heaven and hell are and what they're like. Intention, which makes a human being human, will not budge one iota except for happiness! For intention, per se, is nothing other than the attraction and the carrying out of some love—some form of happiness—for what makes you intend anything has something pleasant, desirable, and satisfying about it. And because intention spurs your intellect to think, no idea comes to mind at all except from the inflowing pleasure of an intention.

"The reason for this is that the Lord, by His influence, activates everything in the souls and minds of angels, spirits, and men. He activates them by the influence of love and wisdom, and this influence is precisely the activity from which all happiness comes. At its source, this is called blessings, fortune, and luck; and in its outcome happiness, well-being, and pleasure. In a broad sense it's called 'good.'

"But the spirits in hell turn everything they have upside down, so they also turn good into evil and truth into untruth. But it still keeps its pleasure, because unless the pleasure remains, there's no motivation, no feeling, and therefore no life.

"These observations show what the happiness of hell is, what it's like, and what it comes from, as well as what the happiness of heaven is, what it's like, and what it comes from."

*When our intentions
are evil, the angels try
to avert our evil ends
and replace them with
good ones.*

<small>ARCANA COELESTIA 5854</small>

After listening to all this, the new spirit was led to the third group, where there were people who inspect results and are called the Facts. They said, "Go down into the world below, and go up into the world above. In the one place you'll observe and feel the happiness of the angels in heaven, and in the other the happiness of the spirits in hell."

But just then the ground opened up at a distance from them, and three devils came up through the opening! They looked as if they were on fire with the happiness of their loves. Those who were with the new spirit could tell that the three devils had come up from hell providentially, so they said to them, "Don't come any closer, but from where you are, tell something about your happiness."

They said, "Everyone, you understand, whether good or bad, has his happiness—a good person the happiness of his goodness, and a bad person the happiness of his badness."

"What's your happiness?" the Facts asked.

They said it was the pleasure of whoring, stealing, cheating, and blaspheming.

Then the Facts asked, "What are those pleasures like?"

The devils said, "To other people they smell like the bad smells from excrement and like the stench of corpses and like the fumes from stagnant urine."

They asked, "Are these smells pleasant to you?"

The devils said, "Very pleasant!"

The Facts said, "Then you're like the filthy creatures that spend their time in things like that."

"If we are, we are," they answered, "but things like that are a joy to our nostrils."

"Anything else?" asked the Facts.

The devils said, "Everyone's allowed to enjoy his own happiness, even the most filthy, as they call it, so long as he doesn't bother good spirits and angels. But with our kind of happiness, we can't help bothering them; so we're thrown into penitentiaries where we suffer dreadfully. The suppression and withholding of our pleasures there is what they call the torment of hell. And it's also an inward agony."

The Facts asked, "Why do you bother good people?"

They said they could not help it. A kind of rage sets in when they see an angel and feel the godly sphere around him.

"You're like wild creatures in this way, too," said the Facts.

When the devils saw the new spirit with angels, a rage soon came over them that looked like the flames of hatred, and so they were thrown back into hell to keep them from doing any harm.

After all this, the angels appeared who view the causes in light of the reasons and the results in light of the causes, and who are in a heaven above the three groups. The angels seemed to be in a brilliant light that circled down in spiral curves. It brought with it a circular wreath of flowers and put it on the new spirit's head, and then a voice came to him from up there, "This laurel wreath is given to you for having thought about heaven and hell from childhood."

From *Conjugial Love* 461

7.

Those who believe that all they need to know about heaven is how to get there find they are mistaken.

An angel and his companions went to a gathering place, where the groups of wise people . . . lingered, and there he gathered the ones who had thought that heavenly joy and eternal happiness are just getting into heaven—getting in by divine grace—and that then their joy is the same as for those in the world who are invited to the palaces of kings on holidays or to weddings.

The angel said to them, "Wait here a while. I'll blow my trumpet, and people who are famous for their wisdom about the spiritual aspects of the church will come."

Some time later nine men came, each wearing laurel, the badge of his reputation. The angel led them into the meeting house where all the people were who had been called together earlier.

In their presence the angel addressed the nine laureates. "I know that in answer to your prayer based on your belief, you've been allowed to go up to heaven and that you returned to this lower ground below heaven with a good idea of the heavenly state. So tell us what heaven seemed like to you."

They answered in turn. "My idea of heaven from early childhood until the end of my life in the world," said the first, "was that it would be a place of all blessedness, happiness, enjoyment, delightfulness, and pleasure; and that if they let me in, those delights would surround me like a halo and I'd freely breathe them in like a bridegroom when he celebrates his wedding and enters the bedroom with his bride. I went up to heaven preoccupied with this idea, and I passed the first guards and the second ones, too. But when I came to the third ones, the officer of the guard challenged me and said, 'Who are you, friend?'

"I answered, 'Isn't this heaven? I came up here in answer to a fervent prayer. Please let me in.' And he did.

"Then I saw angels in white clothes. They walked around me, looked, and murmured, 'What? This new guest doesn't have heavenly clothes on.' I heard it and thought, 'This seems to me like the man the Lord told about who came to a wedding without a wedding garment,' and I said, 'Give me heavenly clothes.' They laughed. Then someone came running from the court with the orders, 'Strip him naked, throw him out, and throw his clothes after him,' and so I was thrown out."

The second said in turn, "I believed as he did, that if I could just get into heaven, which is above my head, joy would surround me and cheer me up forever. I, too, got my wish. But when the angels saw me, they avoided me and said to each other, 'What's this monster? How did this night bird get here?' And I actually felt changed from being human, although I didn't change. It came from breathing the atmosphere of heaven.

"Soon someone ran up from the court with an order for two servants to lead me out, and they led me back by the way I came up, all the way home. And when I came home, I looked human to others and to myself."

The joys of heaven and eternal happiness are from love and wisdom and the conjunction of these is usefulness.

CONJUGIAL LOVE 10

In angels the likeness and image of God clearly appear, since love shines forth in their faces.

DIVINE LOVE AND

WISDOM 358

The third laureate said, "My idea of heaven always involved place, not love; so when I came to this world I longed for heaven with a great yearning, and I saw some people going up and followed them. I got in, though not more than a few steps. But when I tried to consciously enjoy it according to my notion of the joys and blessings there, the light of heaven, which is white as snow (they say it's essentially wisdom), put my mind in a stupor and darkened my eyesight, and I became delirious. And soon, from the heat of heaven, which was in keeping with the dazzling light of the place (they say the heat's essence is love), my heart throbbed, anxiety seized me, an inward pain racked me, and I threw myself on my back on the ground there. And as I lay there, an attendant from the court came with orders to carry me gently away into my own light and heat. Once I came back into them, my mind and heart returned."

The fourth said that he, too, had entertained the idea of heaven as place, not love; and he said, "When I first came into the spiritual world, I asked some wise people whether you could go up to heaven, and they said, 'Anyone may go, but be careful of getting thrown out.'

"I laughed at this and went up, believing like the others that anyone in the whole world can handle the joys there quite fully. But, of course, as soon as I was in, I nearly suffocated; and for the pain and torment it brought to my head and body, I flung myself on the ground and writhed like a snake near a fire. I crawled to a cliff and threw myself down; and afterwards some people standing below picked me up and carried me to a hostel, where my health came back to me."

The other five also told surprising things about their going up to heaven. They compared the altered condition of their life to the condition of fish pulled out of the water into the air and the condition of birds lifted into space. They said that, after their painful experiences, they no longer yearned for heaven but just the common lot of others like themselves, wherever they are.

And they said, "We know that in the world of spirits where we are, everyone is in preparation, the good for heaven and the bad for hell; and when they are ready, they see pathways open for them to communities where there are people like them, whom they will stay with to eternity. And they cheerfully go their ways then, because the paths are the paths of their love."

Everyone from the first assembly who heard these things also admitted that they had had no idea about heaven other than as a place where you drink in, open-mouthed to eternity, the joys that waft around you.

Then the angel with the trumpet said to them, "Now you see that heavenly joy and eternal happiness aren't attributes of a place but of the state of a person's life, and a heavenly state of life comes from love and wisdom. Activity is what brings love and wisdom together, so a heavenly state of life results from uniting love and wisdom in activity—which is the same as saying charity, faith, and good works, since charity is love, faith is the truth that wisdom comes from, and good works are activity. Another thing: in our spiritual world, just as in the natural world, there are places. Otherwise, there would not be homes and individual dwellings. Yet a place here isn't somewhere; it's what seems like somewhere in keeping with a state of love and wisdom, or charity and faith.

"All people who become angels carry their own heavens within them because their heavens are whatever they love. For by creation every person is a tiny model, image, and pattern of heaven at large. The human form is nothing else! So everyone goes to the community in heaven of which he is a detailed model! Consequently, as he enters that community, he is entering a construct just like his own, so he takes part in it as if putting himself in it and it in himself; and he is involved in its life as if it were his own and in his own life as if it were the community's. Each community is like a neighborhood, and the angels there are, so to speak, the interfacing parts that make up the neighborhood.

"Now, this means that people who live by evil ways and the false concepts that come from this have formed a model of hell in themselves; and in heaven this model of hell is in torment under the surge and violent action of opposites against opposites. For hellish love is the opposite of heavenly love, and so the delights of the two loves clash with each other like enemies and kill each other when they meet."

From *Conjugial Love* 10

III

The Marriage
of True Minds

8.

Angels from the highest heaven provide a
glimpse of true married love.

I looked up into the sky one morning and saw vault after vault of
sky above me. I saw the first vault open—the nearest—and then
the second, higher; and finally the third, the highest. By the light
from there, I could tell that on the first vault of sky were angels
from the first or lowest heaven, on the second were angels from
the second or middle heaven, and on the third were angels from
the third or highest heaven.

At first I wondered what this was and why, but soon a voice
like a trumpet sounded from the sky. "We could tell that you're
thinking about married love," it said, "and now we see that you
are, and we understand that as yet no one in the world knows
what the real love in marriage is, as to its source and its essence.
But it's important to know this! That's why the Lord decided to
open the heavens for you, to let a clarifying light flow into your
inner mind so you'll understand. For us in heaven—especially in
the third heaven—our heavenly pleasures are mainly from married love, so we have permission to send down a married couple
for you to see."

Then a chariot could be seen coming down from the highest
or third "sky"! I could see one angel in it; but as it came closer, I
could see two in it. From a distance the chariot gleamed like a

*Those that are in heaven
are continually advanc-
ing toward the spring-
time of life. To grow old
in heaven is to grow
young.*

HEAVEN AND HELL 414

diamond to my eyes, and hitched to it were colts as white as snow. The couple riding in it had two doves in their hands. They called to me, "You want us to come closer. But take care how the glare of the heaven we came down from sinks into you. It's fiery. It will certainly enlighten your higher thoughts, which are heavenly thoughts per se, but you'll not be able to describe them in the world where you are. So what you're about to hear—take it on a rational level and publish it in an understandable rational form."

"I'll be careful," I said. "Come ahead."

They approached, and it was a husband and his wife! "We're married partners," they said. "We've been living happily in heaven since that first period you call the Golden Age, always in the same flower of youth in which you see us today."

I looked each of them over, because I could tell that they must represent married love in its vitality and in its outward splendor—in its vitality in their faces and in its outward splendor in their clothing. For all angels are feelings of love in a human form. Their very most dominant feeling shines out from their faces, and they choose clothes that suit their dispositions. So the saying in heaven is that your disposition clothes you.

In age, the husband looked like someone between adolescence and early adulthood. The sparkling light of his wisdom about love flashed from his eyes, a light that made his face seem to glow from within and the surface of his skin seem to shine with the glow, so that his whole face was a shining ornament. He wore an ankle-length robe with a blue garment under it and belted by a gold sash with three precious stones on it—two sapphires on the sides and a fire-garnet in the middle. His stockings were shining linen with silver thread woven in, and his shoes were all silk. This was a representational expression of married love in the husband.

But in the wife it was represented this way: I saw her face, and I didn't see her face! I saw it as beauty itself, and I didn't see it because this is beyond description. For a flaming brightness was in her face—the kind of light that angels in the third heaven have—and it dulled my vision so that I was somewhat dazzled.

Noticing this, she spoke to me, saying, "What do you see?"

"All I see is married love and what it looks like," I said, "but I see, and I don't see!"

In response, she turned partly away from her husband, and then I could look at her better. Her eyes sparkled with the light of her heaven, which, as I said, is flaming and derives from the love of wisdom there. For the wives in that heaven love their husbands for wisdom and in response to their wisdom, and husbands love their wives for that love and in response to its focus on them; and this is what joins the husbands and wives together.

This gave her such beauty that no painter could try to capture the image of it, since his colors have no such vibrancy nor his art the power to express such beauty. Her hair was done up becomingly to match her beauty, with flowers in it made of diamonds. Her necklace was of fire-garnets with a rose drop of chrysolite, and her bracelets were of large pearls. She wore a scarlet gown with a purple blouse under it, buttoned in front with rubies. I was amazed at how the colors shifted as she looked at her husband and now shone more brilliantly, now less—more when they looked at each other, less when they looked away.

After I had noticed all this, they spoke to me again. Their speech came from such a unity of minds that when the husband spoke it was as if the wife were speaking, too, and when the wife spoke it was as if the husband were speaking, too. I could also hear the sound of married love—inwardly harmonious and springing from delightful states of peace and innocence.

Finally they said, "They're calling us back. We'll be going," and then they again seemed to ride in their chariot as before. It carried them along a paved road among flower gardens from whose beds sprang olive trees and trees full of golden fruit. When they were near their heaven, girls came to meet them, greeted them, and escorted them in.

After this I saw an angel of that heaven, holding in his hand a parchment, which he unrolled, saying, "I noticed that you were thinking about married love. On this parchment are profound secrets about it not yet revealed in the world. They are revealed now because it's relevant. Those unrevealed concepts are more plentiful in our heaven than in others because we participate in the marriage of love and wisdom; but I predict that those whom the Lord invites into the new faith that is the New Jerusalem are precisely the ones who will make this love their own."

The angel dropped the unrolled parchment down. An angelic spirit caught it and laid it on a table in a certain room, which he closed at once. He handed me the key and said, "Write."

From *Conjugial Love* 42

9.

A heavenly couple tells about their love.

I was thinking about the love in marriage, when two naked children appeared in the distance with baskets in their hands and doves flying around them. Up closer they looked as if they were naked and, appropriately, decorated with wreaths of flowers. Little garlands of flowers decorated their heads, and bands of lilies and hyacinth-colored roses, draped crosswise from one shoulder to their waists, ornamented their chests. And round and round both of them was a sort of chain they shared, woven of little leaves with olives worked in.

When they came even closer, they neither looked like babies nor naked but like two people in the flower of youth dressed in robes and shirts of shining silk embroidered with very beautiful flowers. And when they were near me, the warmth of spring breathed on me from heaven through them with a pleasant fragrance like the first blossoms in gardens and fields.

They were two married partners from heaven, and they began to speak to me. I was thinking about the things I had just seen, so they asked, "What did you see?"

I told them that first they looked like naked babies to me, then like babies decorated with garlands, and finally like adults

Everyone who dies in infancy enters heaven, is brought up and instructed there, and becomes an angel.

DIVINE PROVIDENCE 324

wearing clothes embroidered with flowers; and that springtime soon breathed on me with its pleasures.

They laughed good-naturedly at that and said that they had not seemed to themselves like babies as they came, nor naked, nor garlanded, but had looked the same as at present all along. But they said that this was what their married love looked like from a distance—its innocence gave them the look of naked babies, and its pleasures had looked like garlands and now looked like the flowers woven into their robes and shirts.

"You mentioned that the warmth of spring with its pleasant scent of a garden breathed on you as we arrived, so we'll tell you why," they said. "We've been married now for centuries, and we've always been in the flower of youth, as you see us now. At first we were in the state of a young woman and a young man when they first join together in marriage, and we thought this was the ultimate blessing of our life. But we heard from others in our heaven, and later found out for ourselves, that it was a state of heat unseasoned by light and that it's gradually modified as a husband's wisdom matures and a wife loves that wisdom in her husband. This comes about through, and keeps pace with, the things each helps the other take responsibility for in the community. And pleasures arise according to the blend of heat and light—in other words, of wisdom and love for that wisdom.

"When we approached, a warmth like spring breathed on you because married love and the warmth of spring are the same thing in our heaven; for our heat is love, and light united with heat is wisdom, and the things we do are like an atmosphere that surrounds them both. What are heat and light without their surroundings? Likewise, what are love and wisdom without doing anything? No marriage is in them because what they act upon is missing.

"Wherever there is the warmth of spring in heaven, there is real married love. This is because there is spring only where heat and light are together in equal amounts, or where there is as much light as heat and vice versa. And, take it from us, love revels in wisdom and wisdom basks in love, just as heat enjoys light and light heat."

The angel couple went on to say, "For us in heaven there is always daylight and never evening shadows, much less darkness, because our sun doesn't rise and set like your sun but always stays halfway between the zenith and the horizon, which in your language would be 'forty-five degrees in the sky.' This is why the heat and light coming from our sun make a perpetual springtime, and a perpetual spring breeze breathes on those who have love and wisdom together in equal amounts. And what our Lord breathes through the constant combination of heat and light is nothing other than activity! This is also the source of germination in your world and the mating of your birds and animals in springtime, for the warmth of spring opens their more subtle components clear to the most inward, known as their souls. It acts on them, puts its marriage into them, and makes their breeding instinct satisfy itself, due to a steady drive to produce the fruits of activity, which is the propagation of their species.

"But for people the influence of spring warmth from the Lord is constant, so they can enjoy marriage in all seasons, even winter. For men are born vessels for light—that is, wisdom from the Lord—and women are born vessels for heat—that is, love for the man's wisdom from the Lord.

"So now that's why the warmth of spring with its pleasant smell like new blossoms in gardens and fields seemed to breathe on you as we approached."

After this the man offered me his right hand and led me to houses where there were married partners who were in the same flower of youth as he was. He said, "These wives who look like young women now were elderly women in the world, and their husbands who look like young men now were decrepit old men there. The Lord returned them to this blooming youth because they loved each other, and following their religion they avoided adulteries as terrible sins."

He said, "Only those who reject the horrible satisfactions of adultery know the blessed joy of married love. And no one can reject them who doesn't have wisdom from the Lord. No one gets wisdom from the Lord unless he exercises his talents from a love of being active."

Then I also saw the furnishings of their homes. Everything had a heavenly form and shone with gold that seemed to be aflame with the rubies that studded it.

From *Conjugial Love* 137

10.

Swedenborg asks angelic wives about love in marriage.

One morning the sweetest song, which seemed to come from a certain height above me, woke me up; and then I was able to stay for a long time in a spiritual state as if outside my body, in that first consciousness that is more internal, peaceful, and sweet than states later in the day, carefully concentrating on the feeling that the song celebrated. Heavenly singing is nothing other than a mental reaction coming out of the mouth as music. In fact, heavenly singing is the sound of that passionate quality that gives a conversation vitality—minus the conversation.

In that state, I could tell that wives in heaven were setting to music their responses to the pleasures of married love. I could tell that was it by the sound of the song. In it these pleasures found musical expression in wonderful ways.

After this I got up, and I saw into the spiritual world. I looked east, and there, below the sun, there seemed to be golden rain! It was morning dew falling so abundantly that, as the rays of sunshine hit it, it looked to me like a sort of golden rain. More fully awake after this, I went on (in spirit) and asked an angel I happened to meet if he had seen a golden rain coming down from the sun.

The angel answered that he saw it whenever he was thinking about the love in marriage, and then he looked in that direction.

He said, "That shower is falling over a house where there are three husbands with their wives, in a park to the east. The rain seems to be falling above the house from the sun because wisdom about married love and its pleasures is coming down to them— wisdom about married love to the husbands, and wisdom about its pleasures to the wives. But I notice that you're thinking about the pleasures of married love, so I'll take you to the house and introduce you."

He took me through the grounds to houses that were constructed of olive wood and had two cedar posts at the door. He introduced me to the husbands and asked if I could talk with their wives in their presence.

They said I could, and called them.

The wives looked keenly into my eyes, and I asked why.

They said, "We can see exactly what your intention is and from that your feeling, and this tells us what you're thinking about sexual love. We see that you're thinking about it intensely yet chastely." And they said, "What would you like us to tell you about it?"

I said, "Please tell something about the pleasures of married love."

The husbands agreed, saying, "Explain something about them if you care to. His ears are innocent."

The women asked, "Who told you to ask us about the pleasures of that love? Why not ask our husbands?"

I said, "This angel with me told me privately that wives are the vessels and nerve-centers of those pleasures, because wives are loves by birth and all pleasures have to do with love."

The wives answered with smiles on their lips, "Be sensible and don't say such a thing—except ambiguously—because it's wisdom stored deep in the hearts of our sex, and we divulge it to no husband except one with a real love of marriage. There are many reasons, which we keep closely hidden."

The husbands said, "Wives know every state of our minds and don't miss a thing. They see, notice, and feel everything that we give off from our dispositions; but we, on the other hand, know nothing about theirs. Wives are gifted with this talent because they are very delicate forms of love and are what you might call an ardent zeal for the friendship and trust of marriage and the vital happiness of both partners. They take care of this for their husbands and themselves by the wisdom inherent in their love. This wisdom is so prudent that they don't care to—and therefore can't—say that they love, but only that they are loved."

"How do you mean 'don't care to and therefore can't?'" I asked.

They answered that if the least thing like that slipped from women's mouths, a chill would come over their husbands and separate them from bed, bedroom, and sight. "But," the wives said, "this happens to husbands who don't hold marriage sacred and therefore don't love their wives with a spiritual love. It's different for those who do love. The love in their minds is spiritual, and the love in their bodies from this source is physical. We in this dwelling have this physical love from that spiritual love, so we share our private pleasures in married love with our husbands."

I politely asked them to divulge some of these secrets to me, too.

Angels are assigned to infants by the Lord, to care for them.

TRUE CHRISTIAN
RELIGION 677

Angels are sent to people to watch over them and to lead them away from evil affections and thoughts.

They immediately looked out a window to the south, and a white dove appeared, perched on a branch that sprouted an olive. Its wings sparkled as if made of silver, and its head was marked with a cap as if of gold.

As the dove began to spread its wings, the wives said, "We will tell you something. As long as that dove is in sight, it's a sign to us that it's all right."

They said, "Every man has five senses: sight, hearing, smell, taste, and touch. But we have a sixth as well, which is a sense of all the pleasures our husbands find in married love. We have this sense in the palms of our hands when we touch our husbands' chests, arms, hands, or cheeks—especially their chests—and also when they touch us. All the happiness and well-being of the thoughts in their minds, and all the joy and delight in their hearts, and humor and laughter in their breasts come across from them to us, settle in, and we can perceive them, sense them, and feel them. We recognize these as exquisitely and distinctly as your ears recognize the notes in a song and your tongue the flavors of delicacies. In a word, the spiritual pleasures of our husbands take on a physical quality in us, almost as if they wanted a body. So our husbands call us the sensory organs of chaste married love and therefore of its delights. This sixth sense of our gender flourishes, takes hold, stays, and grows in the degree that our husbands love us with wisdom and good judgment and we, in turn, love them for their wisdom and good judgment. In heaven this sixth sense of our gender is called wisdom at play with its love and love at play with its wisdom."

These ideas made me anxious to know more things, such as the kinds of pleasures.

They said, "They're infinite. But we don't want to say any more, so we can't; for the dove in our window with the olive branch under its feet has flown away."

I watched for it to come back, but it was useless. Meanwhile, I asked the husbands, "Don't you have that same sixth sense of married love?"

They answered, "For us it's general, not specific. It's a general happiness, a general joy, and a general well-being from the specific things our wives feel; and the general feeling that we get from them is like a calm peacefulness."

After they said this, we saw through the window a swan perched on a fig branch, and it spread its wings and flew off. Seeing this, the husbands said, "This is a sign for us to stop talking about married love. Come back again, and maybe you'll be shown some more."

They withdrew, and we went away.

From *Conjugial Love* 155b

11.

*Swedenborg experiences a vision of birds and
visits the place where love resides.*

One morning after I had slept, my thoughts plunged into some of
the unknowns about the love in marriage and eventually into this
one: What part of the human mind does married love occupy,
and so what part does marital coldness occupy?

I knew that the human mind has three levels, one above another, and that worldly love occupies the lowest level, spiritual
love the next, and heavenly love the highest; and I knew that there
is a marriage of what is good and what is true on each level. I
knew that goodness is love and truth is wisdom, so there is a marriage of love and wisdom on each level. And this marriage is the
same as a marriage of thinking and intending, because intention
is the vessel of love and thought is the vessel of wisdom.

While I was deep in thought about this, I saw two swans flying north, and soon two birds of paradise flying south, and also
two doves flying east. As I followed their flight with my eye, I saw
the two swans change direction from northward to eastward, and
similarly the two birds of paradise from southward to eastward;
and they all joined the two doves in the east. They flew together
to a high palace there, which was surrounded by olive trees,
palms, and beech trees.

In the palace were three tiers of windows, one above another. As I watched, I saw the swans fly into the palace through open windows in the lowest tier, the birds of paradise through open windows in the middle tier, and the doves through open windows in the highest tier.

An angel stood beside me as I was watching this and he said, "Do you understand these things you've seen?"

I said, "A little bit."

He said, "That palace is a representation of the places that married love occupies in the human mind. The highest part of it, where the doves went, represents the highest level of the mind, which married love occupies as love for goodness coupled with the wisdom of goodness. The middle part, where the birds of paradise went, represents the middle level, which married love occupies as love of the truth coupled with thought related to love of the truth. The lowest part of the palace, where the swans went, represents the lowest level of the mind, which married love occupies as love for what is just and right coupled with the knowledge of what is just and right.

"The three pairs of birds also stand for that—the pair of doves stands for the married love on the highest level, the pair of birds of paradise for the married love on the middle level, and the pair of swans for the married love on the lowest level. The three kinds of trees all around the palace—the olive trees, the palms, and the beech trees—stand for the same things.

"In heaven we call the highest level of the mind heavenly, the middle level spiritual, and the lowest worldly; and we think of them as the stories of a house, one above another, with steps

Every angel is being perfected in wisdom to eternity.

DIVINE PROVIDENCE 334

going up from one to another like a staircase. And each level has, you might say, two rooms, one for love, the other for wisdom, and in front a bedroom, so to speak, where love and its wisdom, or good and its truth, or in other words where intention and its thought are in bed together. The palace allegorically portrays everything you didn't know about married love."

Hearing this, I asked, burning with a desire to see the palace, "Can anyone go in and see it, since it's a symbolic palace?"

"Only people in the third heaven," the angel answered, "because for them every representation of love and wisdom becomes real. They were the ones who told me what I've told you, and also that on the highest level the true love of marriage resides amid mutual love in the thalamus or chamber of intention and amid sensitivity to wisdom in the thalamus or chamber of thought, and they are in bed together in the front bedroom, to the east."

"Why the two chambers?" I asked.

He said, "A husband is in the chamber of thought, and a wife is in the chamber of intention."

I asked, "If married love resides there, where does coldness in marriage reside?"

"Also in the highest level," he said, "but only in the chamber of thought, with the chamber of intention there closed. Whenever it wants to, thought can take its truths up to the highest level, into its chamber, by a spiral stairway. But if intention doesn't take the goodness of its love up to the adjacent room at the same time, this room is shut, and it gets cold in the other one. This is marital coldness. When this coldness toward a wife is there, thought looks down from this highest level to the lowest;

furthermore, if fear doesn't hold it back, it goes down to get warmed by the illicit fire there."

He wanted to tell me more about love in marriage according to the symbols of it in the palace, but he said, "Enough for now. First see if these things are over most people's heads. If they are, why say more? But if not, there is more to reveal."

From *Conjugial Love* 270

IV

Eternal Rest?

12.

Useful activity is contrasted to "eternal rest."

I heard an unusual shout go up from the city of Athens. There was something of laughter in it, something of scorn, and something of regret. Yet that did not make it a shout of conflict, but of accord—not one shout on top of another but one within another. In the spiritual world you can detect the different variety and mixture of feelings in a voice.

"What's going on?" I asked from a distance.

Some people said, "Someone brought word from the place where new arrivals from the Christian world first show up, saying that he heard from three people there that in the world they came from, they, like everyone else, believed that after death 'the Blessed' and 'the Happy' were going to have a rest from work in every way. And since management, duties, and production are work, they thought they would have rest from these. The shout went up because the three newcomers have been brought here by someone we sent for them, and they're waiting outside the gate. In a meeting it was decided not to take them into the Palladium on Parnassus like the previous ones, but to take them into the great auditorium to report their news from the Christian world. Delegates have been appointed to introduce them formally."

I was in a spiritual state. For spirits, distances depend on the

Angels refuse all thanks for the good they do, knowing all that is good and true is from the Lord.

HEAVEN AND HELL 9

state of their feelings, and I felt like seeing and hearing the newcomers, so I found myself right there. I saw them brought in and heard them speaking.

The elders or wiser people were seated at the sides and the others in the middle, and before them was a raised floor. Younger men led the three newcomers and the messenger here in a dignified procession down the middle of the auditorium. When it was quiet one of the young men asked, "What's the news from earth?"

"Plenty is new," they said, "but on what subject, please?"

The elders answered, "What's new from earth about our world and heaven?"

The newcomers answered, "When we entered this world just now, we heard that management, administration, jobs, businesses, scholarship in all the disciplines, and marvelous products exist here and in heaven. And yet we had thought that after going, or being taken, from the natural world into this spiritual world we'd commence eternal rest from work. What are jobs but work?"

The elders said, "Did you think that eternal rest from work meant eternal leisure in which you'd always be sitting or lying down, your heart absorbing pleasures and your mouth sipping joys?"

Smiling sheepishly, the three newcomers admitted, "Something like that."

They were answered, "What do joy, pleasures, and happiness have to do with inactivity? With inactivity the mind deteriorates and doesn't grow. In other words, a person is deadened, not revitalized. Picture someone sitting in complete idleness, hands hanging down, eyes downcast or staring, and picture him surrounded with pleasures at the time. Wouldn't his head and body both get drowsy, and wouldn't the dynamic smile on his face sag? And with every fiber relaxed, wouldn't he nod and sway until he fell on the ground? What keeps your whole organism loose and toned up like a focused mind? And where does mental focus come from unless it comes from carrying out plans and from jobs when done for the joy of it?

"So I'll tell you news from heaven. Management, administration, and higher and lower courts exist there, and so do trades and products."

When the three newcomers heard that there are higher and lower courts in heaven, they said, "Why? Isn't everyone in heaven led and motivated by God, so they know what's just and right? What's the use of judges then?"

A man among the elders answered, "In this world we're taught and we study what's good and true as well as what's just and fair, the same as in the natural world. We don't learn this directly from God, but indirectly from others. And like every person on earth, every angel considers what is true and does what is good as if by his own resources, depending on how imperfect and unrefined the angel's character is. There are the unsophisticated and the wise among angels, too; the wise angels provide judgment when the unsophisticated ones are not sure what is right and lose track of it, in their simplicity and lack of knowledge.

"But since you're still new in this world, come with me if you like, and we'll show you around."

They left the auditorium (some of the elders also went along) and went first to a large library that was divided into smaller libraries by fields of knowledge. The three newcomers were astonished to see all the books and said, "There are even books in this world! Where does the vellum and paper come from? And the pens and ink?"

The older men said, "We can tell that in your former world you thought this world was emptiness because it's spiritual. You thought so because you fostered an idea of spiritual as removed from anything material, and the lack of anything material seemed like nothingness to you and therefore emptiness. Yet this world is full of everything! Everything here is spiritually real, not materially, and material qualities derive from spiritual realities. We who are here are spiritual humans, because we are spiritual substance, not matter. This is why everything in the natural world is here in perfection, even books and written documents and much more."

When the three newcomers heard them call things "spiritually real," they knew it was true, as much because they saw the written books as because they had heard the statement that material qualities derive from spiritual realities.

To convince them further of this, they were taken to the houses of scribes who were transcribing documents written by learned people in the city. The newcomers examined the manuscripts and were astonished at how skillfully these were illuminated.

After this they took the newcomers to museums, schools, seminars, and places where their literary contests were. Some of these were known as games of the Heliconians; others, games of the Parnassians; others, games of the Athenians; and others, games of the Young Women of the Fountain, which they said were so called because young women represent responsiveness to knowledge, and each person's intellect depends on responsiveness to knowledge. The contests under this name were spiritual exercises and debates.

Later they were taken around the city to rulers, administrators, and their officers, who took them to wonderful structures that were made in a spiritual way by tradesmen.

After the newcomers had seen these things, the elder spoke with them again about the eternal rest from work that "the Blessed" and "the Happy" enter after death; and he said, "Eternal rest isn't idleness, because idleness leaves the mind and therefore the whole body listless, sluggish, dull, and sleepy. These qualities are death, not life, much less the eternal life that angels in heaven enjoy. So eternal rest is rest that dispels those qualities and makes a person live. This is nothing other than a rest that boosts your spirits, so it's some effort and product in which the mind is excited, enlivened, and pleased. This happens in the pursuit of some activity that you work for, on, and at.

"For this reason heaven as a whole, from the Lord's point of view, is one continuous activity, and all the angels are angels according to their participation. The joy of usefulness carries them the way a following current does a ship and keeps them always at peace and at ease in peacefulness. This is what eternal rest from work means.

"The fact that an angel is alive according to how eagerly he applies his mind to being active is patently obvious from the fact that each angel is gifted with married love and its vigor, potency, and pleasures according to how he applies himself to the use of his talents."

Once the three newcomers were convinced that eternal rest is not idleness but the joy of some active occupation, some young

Heaven is conjunction with the Lord.

DIVINE PROVIDENCE 20

women came with needlepoint and sewing, their handiwork, and gave it to the newcomers. And as these new spirits went away, the women sang a song with an angelic tune expressing love for useful activities and its pleasures.

From *Conjugial Love* 207

13.

What is heavenly joy?

An angel led the way, and a group followed—those who thought
that heavenly joys are just very pleasant company and agreeable
conversations. The angel led them to groups in the north who, in
the former world, had had that same idea of heavenly joys. There
was a spacious house there, where they were assembled. In the
house were more than fifty rooms, reserved for different kinds of
conversations. In some rooms they talked about things they had
seen and heard in public places and in the streets; in others, they
were telling stories about the different charms of the fair sex,
throwing in more and more witty remarks, until the faces of all
the crowd blossomed into cheerful laughter.

In other rooms they told news about the court, about the
ministries, state policy, and various things that had leaked out of
secret councils; and they discussed events and made conjectures.
In others they talked about business, in others about literary subjects, in others about things related to civic prudence and the
moral life, in others about churches and sects, and so on.

I was able to investigate the house, and I watched people
rushing from room to room looking for others who shared their
interests and their joys. Among the clusters of people I noticed
three types—some catching their breath to speak, some eager to
interview, and some listening greedily.

The Lord's divine providence has for its object a heaven from the human race.

DIVINE PROVIDENCE 27

The house had four doors, one for each direction; and I noticed that a number of people were separating themselves from the crowd, in a hurry to leave. I followed some of them to the east door and saw some people sitting near it with long faces. I stepped up and asked why they were sitting there so depressed.

"The doors of this house are kept shut against escapees," they said. "It's the third day now since we came, and we've tried out the life we longed for of company and conversation. We're so tired of the ceaseless yammering that we can hardly stand to hear the drone of it! So we came to this door in disgust and knocked, but the response was, 'The doors of this house are not exits but entrances. Stay and reap the joys of heaven.' From this answer we gather that we have to stay here forever, which is why depression has settled into our minds. Our chests are starting to tighten up now, and we're getting desperate!"

Then the angel spoke to them. "This condition is *letus gaudiorum*," he said, "the death of your joys. You thought they were the special joys of heaven, but they're only the fringe benefits of heavenly joys."

"So what is heavenly joy?" they asked the angel.

The angel gave this brief answer: "It's the joy in doing something that's of use to yourself and to other people. The joy of usefulness derives its essential quality from love and its outward expression from wisdom. The joy of use, arising from love, via wisdom, is the life and soul of all heavenly joys! They have fabulous parties in heaven that cheer the minds of angels, raise their spirits, delight their hearts, and refresh their bodies; but for them these parties come after they have been useful in their jobs or duties, which are what give life and soul to all their happiness and pleasures. But if that life and soul are missing, the accompanying joys gradually become joyless—quiet at first, then petty, and finally dreary and annoying."

After the angel said this, the door opened. The people sitting there escaped from the house and fled home, each to his occupation and work, and they revived.

From *Conjugial Love* 5

14.

Does heaven consist of festivity?

After this the angel spoke to the ones who had decided that for
them heavenly joy and eternal happiness would be feasts with
Abraham, Isaac, and Jacob, and after the feasts shows and games,
and then more feasts, and so on to eternity.

"Follow me," he said, "and I'll take you to the blessings of
your joys." And he led them through a grove to a platform in a
level place, with tables on it, fifteen on one side and fifteen on
the other.

They asked the angel, "Why so many tables?"

"The first table is Abraham's, the second Isaac's, the third
Jacob's," said the angel, "and next to them are lined up the tables
of the Twelve Apostles. On the other side is the same number of
tables, for their wives. The first three tables are for Sarah, Abraham's wife; Rebecca, Isaac's wife; and Leah and Rachel, Jacob's
wives. The other twelve tables are for the Twelve Apostles' wives."

After a little wait, we saw all the tables loaded with platters
placed between little ornamental pyramids of delicacies. The
guests stood around them waiting to see the heads of the tables.
In a while they arrived as expected, filing in, from Abraham to the
last apostle. Soon each approached his own table and settled onto

a couch at the head of it, and then they told the standing group, "Settle back like us."

They did—the men with the Fathers and the women with their wives—and ate and drank gladly, and with reverence.

After dinner the Fathers went away, and then began the sports, the dances of young women and men, and after them the performances.

When it was over, they were invited to feast again, but with the stipulation that the first day they would eat with Abraham, the second with Isaac, the third with Jacob, the fourth with Peter, the fifth with James, the sixth with John, the seventh with Paul, and with the rest in order until the fifteenth day, when the feasting would start over again in the same order, and so on to eternity.

Now the angel called together the men in the group and said to them, "All the people you saw at the tables had the same unreal concept as you about the joys of heaven and the eternal happiness one gains from those joys. To let them see how unreal their ideas were and to lead them away from those notions, the Lord set up and permitted those mock feasts.

"Those leaders you saw at the heads of the tables were aged impersonators—simpletons, mostly—who were prouder than others because they had beards and some wealth, which induced the fantasy that they were the ancient Fathers. But follow me. I'll show you the way out of this gymnasium."

They followed and saw fifty people here and fifty there who had stuffed their bellies with food to the point of nausea and badly wanted to return to familiar home surroundings—some to

Every good and true thing inspired by the angels is of the Lord; thus the Lord is continually speaking with us.

ARCANA COELESTIA 904

their duties, some to their businesses, and some to their work. But the attendants in the grove detained many of them and asked about their days of feasting and whether they had dined at the tables with Peter yet, and with Paul, saying that, if they left before doing so, it would be improper and would disgrace them.

But most of them answered, "We're fed up with our joys! Food has lost its flavor for us! Our pleasure in it is burned out! We can't bear to taste it! We've dragged through several days and nights of this indulgence, and we plead desperately to be let out!" And when they were set free, they fled home at a dead run, gasping for breath.

Then the angel called together the men in the group; and on the way, he taught them these things about heaven: "There's food and drink in heaven, the same as in the world. There are parties and feasts. And for the leaders there, there are tables with splendid meals on them, delicacies, and luxuries, which cheer and refresh their hearts. And there are also games and performances and musicals and songs—all in the highest perfection. These things contribute to joy but are not happiness, which is in joy and therefore comes from joy. The happiness in joy is what makes it joy, enriches it, and keeps it from fading and becoming distasteful. And everyone has this happiness from the usefulness in what he does.

"Tucked away in an angel's inclinations is a natural bent that attracts his or her mind to something that needs to be done and that soothes and satisfies his or her mind. This serenity and satisfaction produce a mental state that can receive from the Lord a love of being useful. From receiving this comes heavenly happiness, which is the vital element in those joys that I mentioned before.

"Heavenly food in essence is nothing but love, wisdom, and usefulness together—in other words, usefulness through wisdom, due to love. On account of this, a person in heaven gets food for the body according to the useful things he or she does—magnificent food for people who are useful on a large scale, plain but very delicious for those engaged in average usefulness, common food for those who do common work, and none for the inactive."

From *Conjugial Love* 6

V

Spiritual Essence

15.

At the Temple of Wisdom, Swedenborg
learns about the qualities of women.

Once I was talking with some angels in the spiritual world when I
had the happy inspiration of wanting to see the Temple of
Wisdom, which I had seen once before, and I asked the angels
about the way there.

The angels said, "Follow the daylight, and you'll get there."

I said, "What do you mean, 'follow the daylight?' "

They said, "Our light gets brighter and brighter as you ap-
proach the Temple of Wisdom, so you keep going where there's
more light. See, our light comes from the Lord, who is our sun;
and He, after all, is the source of wisdom."

Then, with two of the angels, I followed the increasing daylight, climbing a steep path to the top of a hill to the south. There
was an elaborate gate there, and the gate keeper opened it when
he saw me with the angels. We saw a corridor of palm and laurel
trees, which we followed. The corridor circled around and ended
in a garden, in which was the Temple of Wisdom.

As I looked around I saw smaller shrines that resembled the
temple, with wise people in them. We went up to one of the
shrines, and at the entrance we spoke with its occupant, telling
why we came and how we got there. He said, "Welcome! Come in.
Sit down. We'll visit and chat about wisdom."

The angels are continually being perfected.

ARCANA COELESTIA 3308

I looked around inside the shrine. It was divided into two parts but was still one shrine. A transparent partition was what divided it in two; but the transparency, like the purest crystal, made it seem like one structure. I asked about this.

"I'm not alone," he said. "My wife is with me, and we're two and yet not two but one flesh."

But I said, "I know you're a wise man," and I said, "How do being wise and wisdom relate to a woman?"

At this our host made an almost scornful face and threw up his hands, and then other wise men arrived from the nearby shrines. He said to them jokingly, "Our visitor here wants to know, 'How do being wise and wisdom relate to a woman?'"

They all laughed at this and said, "What being wise and wisdom are there without a woman—or without love? A wife is the element of love in a wise man's wisdom!"

But our host said, "Now let's visit with a little chat about wisdom. Let's talk about reasons why, in this case, reasons for the female gender's beauty."

They spoke one after the other, and the first gave this reason: that the Lord makes women sensitive to men's wisdom, and sensitivity to wisdom is beauty itself.

The second man gave this reason: that the Lord made woman from man's wisdom (because He created her from man), and so she is the embodiment of wisdom animated by a feeling of love; and a feeling of love is life itself, so woman is the spark of life in wisdom, while a man is the wisdom. The vitality in wisdom is beauty itself.

The third gave this reason that women are beautiful: that

women are endowed with an appreciation for the pleasures of married love, and their entire body is an organ of this appreciation, so as the habitat of married love's pleasures and the appreciation of them, women can't help being beauty.

The fourth gave this reason: that the Lord took the beauty and grace of life away from man and transplanted it into woman; so unless man is reunited with his beauty and grace in woman, he's stern, rigid, dry, and repulsive, and he's not wise except for his own personal advantage, which is stupid. But when, in a wife, a man is reunited with the beauty and grace of his life, he gets a sense of humor and becomes attractive, has vitality, and is loveable; and so he's wise.

The fifth wise man gave this reason: that women are not created beautiful for their own sake but to soften men's inherent hardness, lighten their inherently serious nature, and warm their naturally cold hearts. And this happens when men become one flesh with their wives.

The sixth gave this reason: that the universe created by the Lord is an absolutely perfect work, but nothing in it has been created more perfect than the beautiful appearance and charming manner of a woman, so a man can give thanks to the Lord for that gift and repay it by accepting wisdom from Him.

After these things and other similar things had been said, our host's wife appeared through the transparent partition, and she said to her husband, "Please say something." When he spoke, we noticed the vitality of wisdom from his wife in what he said, for her love was in the sound of his voice. So the fact was verified by an experiment.

When after death people become angels, they are in inexpressible intelligence and wisdom compared to the intelligence and wisdom they had while they lived in the world.

HEAVEN AND HELL 576

After this we explored the Temple of Wisdom, as well as the grounds around it, came away filled with happiness, went down the corridor of trees to the gate, and descended the path we had come up.

From *Conjugial Love* 56

16.

Angelic wives talk about wisdom.

I once looked out the window to the east and saw seven women lingering over a bed of roses by a spring, drinking the water. I focused my eyes and looked hard to see what they were doing. They could tell I was staring at them, so one of them beckoned me, and I left the house and hurried over to them. As I approached, I politely asked them where they were from.

"We're wives," they said, "and we're here talking about the joy of married love. For various reasons we've settled it that the pleasures of married love are also the pleasures of wisdom."

This answer so intrigued my mind that I could see it was a spiritual experience, and I, therefore, had deeper and clearer perception than ever before. So I said to them, "Let's get each other's opinions about these pleasures." They nodded "yes," and I asked, "How do you wives know that the pleasures of married love are the same as the pleasures of wisdom?"

"We know it from the interrelationship of the wisdom in our husbands with the pleasures of married love in ourselves," they said, "because our pleasures from this love ebb and flow and take their whole character according to the wisdom in our husbands."

When I heard this, I asked, "I know that you respond to your husbands' sweet talk and their wittiness and that you delight in it

*Heavenly joy is so
great as to be beyond
description.*

HEAVEN AND HELL 409

with all your heart. But I'm surprised that you say their wisdom does this. Tell me—what wisdom and what kind of wisdom?"

The wives answered my questions with impatience. "You don't think we know what wisdom and what kind of wisdom; yet our attention is always on the wisdom in our husbands, and we study it every day in their own words. For from dawn to dusk we wives have our husbands' attitudes in mind. There's hardly a gap of one minute in the day when we don't have an intuitive insight into their attitudes or are distracted from them. (Husbands, on the other hand, are rarely aware of our attitudes during the day.) So this is why we know what kind of wisdom in them finds pleasure in us. Husbands call it the wisdom of spiritual thought and spiritual behavior. They say that the wisdom of spiritual thought has to do with understanding and knowing, and they say that the wisdom of spiritual behavior has to do with your intentions and how you live. They combine both wisdoms into one wisdom and say that its delights translate from their minds into joy in our hearts and from our hearts into their hearts, and so the pleasures come back to the wisdom they came from!"

And then I asked, "Do you know something else about husbands' wisdom finding happiness in you?"

"We do," they said. "There is spiritual wisdom. The wisdom of thought and the wisdom of behavior come from it. Spiritual wisdom is to acknowledge the Lord our Savior as the God of heaven and earth and obtain spiritual truths from Him—which is done through the Word and through instruction from it. This is where spiritual thought comes from. Spiritual behavior comes from living by spiritual thought, with the Lord's help. Our husbands call these two things—spiritual thought and behavior—the overall wisdom that activates the real love in marriage.

"We've also heard from them the reason that this wisdom opens the innermost parts of their minds and therefore of their bodies, providing a free passage for love to flow from its headwaters to its outlets. The life of married love depends on the strong, plentiful flow of this 'stream.'

"The wisdom of spiritual thought and behavior in our husbands has a specific purpose and scope in marriage—to love only a wife and to reject every selfish desire for anyone else—and to the extent that it succeeds, the love reaches a higher level and greater perfection. And it also gives us that much more special and exquisite feelings of delight in response to the joy of our husbands' feelings and the happiness of their thoughts."

Next I asked if they knew how this sharing works.

"Every relationship through love takes stimulation, invitation, and response," they said. "The appealing stance of our love is something happening, or a stimulus. The state of wisdom in our husbands is receptive, or an invitation, and is also recognizably reactive, or a response. We feel this response with heartfelt joy, in keeping with our state of mind. Our state of mind is always open and ready to accept anything at all which is consistent with, and comes from, the morality in our husbands and which, therefore, is also consistent with the state of love standing by in us."

The women also said, "Be careful you don't take the pleasures we've been talking about to mean the more outward pleasures of this love. We never say anything about these, but about the joy in our hearts that always corresponds to the state of our husbands' wisdom."

After this a flying dove with the leaf of a tree in its beak seemed to appear in the distance. But as it approached it turned out to be a little boy instead of a dove, with a piece of paper in his hand. Coming up to us he held the paper out to me and said, "Read this in the presence of the virgins of the spring."

And I read these words, "Tell the Earthdwellers you are with that genuine married love does exist. It has thousands of pleasures, and the world still knows hardly any of them. But it will recognize them when the church betroths herself to the Lord and marries."

Then I asked, "Why did the boy call you virgins of the spring?"

"We are called virgins when we are near this spring," they answered, "because affection for the truths of our husbands' wisdom is what we are, and affection for truth is called a virgin. Also, a spring stands for the truth of wisdom, and the rose garden we are in stands for the pleasures of wisdom."

Then one of the seven women wove a wreath of roses, sprinkled it with spring water, put it on the boy's cap, around his little head, and said, "Have the pleasures of knowledge. You see, that cap stands for knowledge, and a wreath from this rose bed is the joy of it."

Decorated this way, the boy set off, and in the distance he again looked like a dove flying, but with a garland on its head.

From *Conjugial Love* 293

Spirits who think that heaven consists of eternal
praise learn what such a place would be like.

An angel guide went into a hall, to the people who were firmly
convinced that heavenly joy and eternal happiness are uninterrupted glorification of God and a religious festival year after year
to eternity, because they had thought, in the world, that in heaven
they would see God, and because, on account of the worship of
God, heavenly life is called a perpetual sabbath.

The angel said to these people, "Follow me, and I'll lead you
to your joy," and took them into a small city where there was a
church and all the buildings were known as holy shrines.

In the city they saw people streaming in from every corner of
the surrounding country, and among them a number of priests
who received the new arrivals, greeted them, and led them by the
hand to the gates of the church and from there into some of the
buildings around the church, and introduced them into the perpetual worship of God.

The priests were saying, "This city is an entryway to heaven,
and the city's church is the passage to a magnificent and very spacious church in heaven where the angels glorify God with prayers
and praises to eternity. The regulations, both here and in heaven,

are that you first go to church and stay for three days and three nights. After this initiation, you go in groups to the buildings of this city, which are all shrines we have consecrated, to pray, shout, and preach from building to building. Be especially careful not to think to yourself or say to your companions anything but what is holy, pious, and worshipful."

Then the angel led his group into the church, which was packed full with many who had enjoyed great honor in the world and many ordinary people, too. There were guards posted at the doors to keep anyone from going out before staying the three days.

The angel said, "This is the second day since these people came in. Look them over, and you'll see their glorification of God."

The visitors looked around and saw most of the congregation sleeping and those who were awake yawning again and again. Some of them looked like out-of-the-body forms due to their thoughts being raised continually to God and never drifting back to their bodies. That was how they seemed to themselves and therefore to others. Some seemed wild-eyed from their unrelenting self-control. In a word, all of them were tight-chested, heartsick from boredom, shrinking back from the pulpit, and shouting, "Our ears are getting numb! Stop preaching! We can't listen to your voice anymore! The sound is beginning to make us cringe!"

Then they got up and rushed en masse to the doors, burst them open, and pushed into the guards, driving them away.

When the priests saw this, they followed the worshipers and stuck close beside them, preaching on and on, praying, sighing, and saying, "Celebrate the festival! Glorify God! Be holy! In this entryway to heaven we're going to introduce you to eternal glorification of God in a huge, magnificent church in heaven, and it will bring you the eternal enjoyment of happiness!"

But these words did not register with the worshipers, who scarcely heard them for the stupor induced by two days of uplifting their minds and staying away from their activities at home and at work. When they tried to get away from the priests, the priests grabbed them by the arms, and by the clothing, too, pushing them toward the buildings to witness there. It was no use. They shouted, "Let go of us! We feel physically like we're going to pass out!"

After this exchange, four men with white robes and miters appeared. One of them had been an archbishop in the world, and the other three had been bishops. Now they had become angels. They called the priests together and spoke to them. "We saw you from heaven with these sheep," they said. "How you feed them! You feed them to insanity! You don't know what glorification of God means. It means to bear the fruits of love. That is, to do the work of your occupation faithfully, sincerely, and intently, for this is love of God and love of your neighbor. This is the bond and fulfillment of society. God is glorified by this, and then by worship at the appropriate times. Haven't you read the Lord's words? 'My Father is glorified in the fact that you bear fruit, and you will become My disciples' (John 15:8). You, as priests, can glorify in

There are two angels with each of us, one to affect what is of our will and the other to affect what is of our understanding.

ARCANA COELESTIA 5978

worship because it is your occupation; and you get honor, fame, and pay for it. But if the honor, fame, and pay weren't part and parcel of your occupation, you couldn't keep this glorification up any more than they can."

After this advice, the bishops ordered the doorkeepers, "Let everyone go in and out, because it's a crowd who can't imagine any other heavenly joy than perpetual worship of God, since they don't know anything about what heaven is like."

From *Conjugial Love* 9

VI

The Source

Angels debate with evil spirits about the existence of God.

One morning after I first woke up, before I was completely awake, I was meditating in an early morning light that was clear and serene, when I saw out the window what looked like a flash of lightning, and soon heard something sounding like thunder. As I was trying to figure out what could have caused it, I heard from heaven that there were some spirits not far from me who were having a fierce argument about which one—God or nature—is the supreme power. The light flashing like lightning and the air exploding like thunder were symbols and manifestations of the two sides of the argument battling and colliding, one in favor of God, the other in favor of nature.

This spiritual battle had begun in the following way: Some evil spirits in hell said to each other, "I wish we could talk face to face with angels from heaven. We could utterly and completely show them that what they call God, the source of all things, is just nature. 'God' is only a word, unless they really mean nature." And because the evil spirits believed this point of view with all their heart and soul and because they longed to talk face to face with angels from heaven, they were given permission to ascend out of the mud and darkness of hell and talk to two angels who were then coming down from heaven. This was in the world of spirits, which is midway between heaven and hell.

Upon first seeing the angels there, the evil spirits began shouting out in a furious voice, "Are you the angels from heaven we are allowed to argue with about God and nature? You know, because you acknowledge God, you have the reputation of being wise, but you are really so naive. Who has seen God? Who understands what God is? Who really comprehends the idea that God can and does govern the universe and each and every thing in it? Who but some joe-on-the-street would believe in something he can't see or understand? What could be more obvious than the fact that nature is all there is? Who has seen anything but nature with his own eyes? Who has heard anything but nature with his own ears? Who has smelled anything but nature with his nose? Who has tasted anything but nature with his tongue? Who has felt anything but nature with his hands and body? Aren't our bodily senses witnesses to truth? On their testimony, who wouldn't swear that what we are saying is right? Isn't our breathing a witness, the very source of our physical life? What else do we breathe except nature? For all of us, aren't our heads part of nature? Where could the thoughts in our heads flow in from except nature? If you took away nature, could you think at all?" And many other arguments made from the same batter.

On hearing all this the angels replied, "You talk this way because you only function on the level of your senses. All spirits in hell have their thinking immersed in their bodily senses and can't lift their minds above that level, so we forgive you. Living an evil life and having the accompanying false belief system has closed off the inner realms of your minds so much that elevation above the level of the senses is impossible for you, except when you're temporarily suspended from evil living and false beliefs. On hearing the truth, an evil spirit is able to understand it as well as any angel, but he doesn't retain it because his own evil obliterates it and substitutes something false. But we can tell that you're in a suspended state now, and therefore you can understand the truth of what we are saying. So consider the points we are about to make."

And the angels said, "You have lived and died in the natural world, and now you are in the spiritual world. Before now, you didn't know anything about a life after death, did you? Isn't it true that you denied it before, and put yourselves on a par with animals? You didn't know anything about heaven and hell before, did you? Or anything about the heat and light in this spiritual world? Or that you are no longer in nature but above it? You see, this world is spiritual, and everything about it is spiritual; and what is spiritual is so much higher than what is natural that not even the least bit of nature, where you used to be, could flow into this world. But because you held nature to be a god or a goddess, you believe that this world's light and heat are the light and heat of the natural world, when they aren't at all. Nature's light is darkness here, and its heat is coldness. You didn't know anything, did you, about the sun of this world, the source of our light and heat? You didn't know that this sun is pure love and that the sun of the natural world is pure fire; and the world's sun, which is pure fire, enables nature to exist and subsist, while the sun of heaven, which is pure love, enables life itself, which is love together with wisdom, to exist and subsist. Therefore, nature, which you make a god or a goddess, is clearly dead.

"If you are given protection, you can come up with us into heaven; and if we are given protection, we can go down with you into hell. What you'll see in heaven is awe-inspiring and dazzling,

In heaven are those who lived in the world in heavenly love and belief.

HEAVEN AND HELL 311

but what you'll see in hell is disgusting and polluted. This contrast exists because all those in heaven worship the Lord and all those in hell worship nature. The things you'll see in the heavens are awe-inspiring and dazzling because they correspond to feelings of love for what is good and true. The things you'll see in hell are disgusting and polluted because they correspond to feelings of love for what is evil and false. Now, from everything we've said, you decide which one, God or nature, is truly all there is."

The evil spirits' answer to this was, "In our current state we can conclude that the answer is God; but when our minds are obsessed with evil delight, we only see nature."

The two angels and the evil spirits were standing not far from me, so I saw them and heard them. And strange to say, I saw around them many spirits who had been distinguished scholars in the natural world. I was amazed that the scholars would at one point stand next to the angels, then later next to the evil spirits, and would agree with whoever they were close to. I was told, "They change locations as their minds change sides, favoring one side at one time, the other side at another, because they're as fickle as Vertumnus, the god of change, in their beliefs. And we'll tell you a secret: we looked down into the world to examine its distinguished scholars and found sixty percent in favor of nature, and the rest in favor of God—and the latter came out in favor of God not because they understood but because they frequently merely repeated what they had heard about nature being from God. Their frequent talk from memory and remembrance, although it does not come from any accompanying thought or intelligence, still brings about an outward appearance of belief."

Afterwards the evil spirits were given protection and went up with the two angels into heaven. They saw the awe-inspiring and dazzling things that are there. At the time, enlightened by the light of heaven there, they acknowledged that there is a God, that nature was created to serve the life force that comes from God, and that nature in itself is dead and, therefore, does nothing on its own but is acted upon by the life force. After having these visions and perceptions, they came back down. As they were descending, their love for doing evil returned and closed off their intellect at the top and opened it at the bottom; and then above it there appeared a shadow flashing like lightning with hellish fire. And right away when their feet touched the earth, the ground yawned open under them, and they fell back down towards their own kind.

From *True Christian Religion 77*

19.

Where does the soul's delight come from?

An angel went to a house where the wise people from the Christian world were convened, and he gathered up the ones who had adopted the belief that the joy of heaven and eternal happiness are the pleasures of a nature park. "Follow me," he said, "and I'll lead you into paradise—your heaven—to begin the blessings of your eternal happiness."

He led them through a lofty gateway made from the limbs and branches of stately trees twined together. Once inside, he led them in a roundabout way from one place to another. It actually was an informal garden in the first entrance to heaven, where they send people who believed, while in the world, that heaven is all one park, because it is called paradise—people who had the notion impressed on them that after death comes total rest from labor and that this rest is nothing other than inhaling breezes of delight, walking on roses, cheered by the most delicious grape juice, and having festive banquets; and that this life is to be found only in a heavenly Eden.

Led by the angel, they saw a great crowd of old and young men, boys, women, and girls, sitting three-by-three and ten-by-ten in rose gardens, weaving garlands to deck the heads of the old men and arms of the young men and to twine around the chests of the boys. They saw others gathering fruit from the trees and taking it to their friends in osier baskets, others pressing the juice of grapes, cherries, and berries into cups and merrily drinking it; others sniffing the fragrances that the flowers, fruits, and aromatic leaves gave off all around; others singing sweet songs to charm the ears of anyone around; others sitting at fountains making the water squirt from the ducts in various shapes; others walking around talking and tossing off pleasantries; others running, playing, and dancing, here in rhythm and there in circles; others going into little garden houses to relax on the couches. And there were many other paradisal delights.

After the angel's group had seen these things, he led them around here and there and at last to some people sitting in a very beautiful rose garden surrounded by olive, orange, and citron trees. They were rocking back and forth with their hands to their cheeks, wailing and weeping. The angel's followers spoke to them and said, "Why are you sitting like that?"

"It's the seventh day now since we entered this Paradise," they answered. "When we got here, it seemed as if our minds were raised into heaven and placed in the deepest happiness of its joy. But after three days the edge began to wear off this happiness. It faded from our minds and feelings till it was no happiness at all. And when our imagined joys ended like this we began to fear we had lost all pleasure from our life. We're becoming skeptical about eternal happiness—if there is such a thing.

"Then we wandered the paths and clearings looking for the gate where we came in, but we were wandering round and round in circles.

The more we love what is good and what is true the more angels love to be with us.

Arcana Coelestia 1740

"We asked people we met. Some of them said, `You won't find the gate, because this nature park is a great big labyrinth, the kind where anyone who wants to get out gets deeper in. So there's nothing to do but stay here forever. You're in the middle of it, the center of all its delights.'"

The despairing people said, further, to the angel's group, "We've been sitting here for a day and a half now. With no hope of finding the way out, we sat down in this rose garden; and we see plenty of olives, grapes, oranges, and citrons around us. But the more we look at them the more tired our eyes are of seeing, our noses of smelling, and our mouths of tasting. This is why you see us in sorrow, grief, and tears."

When the group's angel heard this, he said, "This labyrinth or park really is an entrance to heaven. I know the way, and I'll lead you out."

When the angel said this, the people sitting there stood up and hugged him and joined his group and followed him. On the way, the angel taught them about heavenly joy and its eternal happiness—that these are not the superficial delights of Paradise unless the inward delights of Paradise are there within them at the same time. "The outward delights of Paradise are only de-lights for the body's senses, but the inward delights of Paradise are delights of the feelings in your soul. The outward delights have no soul, so the life of heaven is not in them unless the in-ward delights are in them. And any delight without soul related to it gradually gets feeble and dull and is more tiring to the mind than work. There are garden paradises all over heaven, and the angels get pleasure from them, too, and they enjoy the pleasures just to the extent that the delight of their soul is in them."

"What's the delight of a soul?" everyone asked when they heard this, "and where does it come from?"

"The delight of a soul comes from love and wisdom from the Lord," the angel answered. "Love is the motive force, and it acts through wisdom; so you find both love and wisdom in what love and wisdom do, and what they do is something of use. This delight flows from the Lord into your soul and works down through the higher and lower levels of your mind into all your bodily senses, and there it is fulfilled. This is what makes joy really joy, and makes it eternal—from the Eternal, from whom it comes. You've seen something of a paradise, and I assure you that not one thing is there, not even a leaf, that is not from a marriage of love and wisdom in usefulness. So if a person has this marriage in him, he is in the paradise of heaven—in other words, in heaven."

From *Conjugial Love* 8

20.

After hearing two angels discuss the nature of love, wisdom, and usefulness, Swedenborg enters the Temple of Wisdom.

One morning as I woke up from sleep I saw two angels coming down from heaven, one from the southern part of heaven and one from the eastern part. They were both in carriages to which white horses were harnessed. The carriage carrying the angel from the southern part of heaven gleamed as if were made of silver, and the one carrying the angel from the eastern part of heaven gleamed as if it were made of gold. And the reins they both held in their hands were glowing like the flame-colored light of dawn. That is how they looked from a distance; but as they drew closer they did not look like they were in a carriage but looked like angels, that is, like human beings. The one who came from the eastern part of heaven wore clothing of a radiant purple, and the one who came from the southern part of heaven wore clothing of a radiant hyacinth blue. When they were below the heavens in the lower regions, they ran towards each other as if each were racing to be first, and they hugged and kissed each other.

I heard that, when they had lived in the world, these two angels had formed a bond of deep friendship, but now one was in the eastern heaven and one in the southern heaven. In the eastern heaven are those who have love from the Lord, while in the southern heaven are those who have wisdom from the Lord. After they spoke for a while about the magnificent things in their respective heavens, a question came up in their conversation about whether heaven is essentially love or wisdom. They agreed right away that one comes from the other but debated which one is the origin of which. The angel from the heaven of wisdom asked the other what love is. The other angel replied, "Love has to come from the Lord as the sun. It is the vital heat of both angels and people on earth. It is their life. Love gives rise to what are called feelings, which, in turn, produce perceptions and, finally, thoughts. A conclusion flows from this that wisdom starts out as love. Consequently, thought starts out in the form of a feeling from that love. By examining carefully how one thing leads to another, you can see that a thought is nothing else but the manifestation of a feeling. This is not generally recognized because thoughts relate to light but feelings to heat; therefore, it is easy to focus on thoughts but not on feelings, just as it is easier to focus on what someone is saying than on the tone of his voice.

"An analogy with speech and tone of voice can show that thought is, in fact, nothing but a feeling taking on a form, for speech is nothing but a tone of voice taking on the form of words. This is a true simile, too, because the tone of voice conveys the feeling and the speech the thought; therefore, the feeling intones and the thought speaks. My point would become even clearer if I said, 'Taking sound away from speech leaves no speech, right? Likewise taking the feeling away from thought leaves no thought.' So everything in wisdom is really love; that should be clear by this point. As a result the essence of the heavens is love; their manifestation is wisdom. Or, to put it another

The thoughts of angels are not limited and confined by ideas from time and space.

HEAVEN AND HELL 266

The purpose of the cre-
ation of the universe is
an angelic heaven from
the human race.

DIVINE LOVE AND WISDOM

329

way, the heavens take their substance from divine love and their form from divine love through divine wisdom. As we agreed earlier, one does indeed belong to the other."

At that point there was a newly arrived spirit with me who, at hearing all this, asked whether their simile works with charity and so on, in that charity has to do with feelings and faith has to do with thoughts.

The angel replied, "It is very much the same situation. Faith is nothing but a manifestation of charity, as plainly as speech gives form to the tone of voice. Faith is, in fact, formed from charity the way speech is formed from tone of voice. We in heaven have even researched the mode of formation, but there is no room to go into that here."

He added, "Now, by faith I mean a spiritual faith, whose spirit and life come solely from charity. For true charity is spiritual, and because that is so, the faith becomes spiritual too. Faith without charity is a merely natural faith, which is really a dead faith; it goes hand in hand with merely natural states of feeling, also known as cravings."

The angels were, of course, talking spiritually about all this. Spiritual speech interweaves thousands of nuances that natural language cannot express and that, amazing to say, cannot even fall into the ideas of natural thought.

So I ask you, please hang onto these concepts; and when you come from natural light into spiritual light, which happens after death, then ask what faith is and what charity is, and you will see clearly that faith is charity taking form; therefore, everything within faith is really charity. Charity is the soul, life, and essence of faith, just the way feeling is the soul, life, and essence of

thought and the tone is the soul, life, and essence of speech. And
if you have a desire to, you will see charity being molded into
faith much the way someone's tone of voice is molded into artic-
ulate speech, since the two pairs correspond to each other.

After the angels had said all of the above, they went away. And
as they left, each to his own heaven, stars appeared around their
heads. And when they had reached a good distance away from
me, they looked once again as if they were in carriages as before.

After the two angels were beyond my range of vision, I saw a
garden to my right with olive trees, grapevines, fig trees, laurel,
and palm trees planted in order according to their inner meaning. I looked closer and saw angels and spirits walking and talking
among the trees. Then an angelic spirit returned my gaze. ("Angelic spirits" is the term for those in the world of spirits who are
prepared for heaven and afterwards become angels.) The spirit
came from the garden towards me and asked, "Do you want to
come with me into our paradise? You are going to hear and see
amazing things!" I went off with him. Then he said to me, "All
these whom you see here (for there were many) have a love for
truth, and are, therefore, in the light of wisdom. There is also a
building here that we call the Temple of Wisdom. But you cannot
see it if you think you are rather wise; still less if you feel satisfied
with your state of wisdom; and not at all if you think your wisdom comes from yourself. This is because those attitudes block
you from receiving the light of heaven with a love for genuine
wisdom. Genuine wisdom is seeing from the light of heaven that
what you know and understand and are aware of is like a drop, or
almost nothing, compared to the ocean of what you do not know
or understand and are not aware of. All in this paradisal garden

who acknowledge from self-awareness and perception that they are that relatively unwise—they all see the Temple of Wisdom." Inner light allows you to see it. Outer light by itself does not.

And because I had often thought this—long ago I knew it, then later I perceived it, and finally by seeing it in an inner light I acknowledged that humankind is so unwise—lo and behold, I was given the ability to see the temple. It had an amazing form. It was raised up off the ground, a square, with walls of crystal, an elegantly arched ceiling of translucent jasper stone, and foundation made out of various precious stones. There were steps of polished alabaster leading up into it. Beside the steps on either side, there appeared something like lions with their cubs.

And then I asked whether I was allowed to go in, and the reply was "yes." So I went up; and as I entered I saw something like cherubs flying just below the ceiling, but they soon faded away. The floor I was walking on was made out of cedar, and the translucent walls and ceiling gave the whole temple the form of light.

The angelic spirit came in with me, so I relayed to him what I had heard from the two angels about love and wisdom and about charity and faith. And he said, "Did they also mention the third thing?"

"What third thing?" I asked.

He replied, "It is usefulness. Love and wisdom without usefulness are nothing. They are only abstract entities. They do not become real before they exist in useful activity. For love, wisdom, and usefulness are three things that cannot be separated. If they are separated, each becomes nothing. Love is not anything without wisdom; only in wisdom is it formed into anything, and the thing it is formed into is usefulness. Therefore, when love comes through wisdom into usefulness, it becomes something; in fact, it then really exists for the first time. These three are just like a goal, an impetus, and an effect; the goal is nothing unless an impetus brings it into effect. If any of the three links is broken, the whole chain is broken and becomes practically nothing. The same goes for charity, faith, and good works. Charity without faith is nothing; neither is faith without charity. And faith and charity are nothing without good works; but in good works, they become something and take their quality from how useful the good works are. The same goes for love, thought, and work; and for the will, the intellect, and action. All this becomes clear to see in this temple, because the light we are in here is one that enlightens the inner reaches of the mind. So nothing is complete or perfect unless it has this trinity, as you can see from geometry. For a line does not really exist unless it is drawn out to become an area; and an area does not really exist except in reference to a three-dimensional body. Therefore, one leads to the next in order to exist, and to coexist in the third. As it is with this, so it is with every single created thing: everything becomes complete in its third aspect. You can see why the number 'three' in the Word can be understood spiritually to mean 'complete and total.' Given all this, I cannot help but be amazed that some people profess faith alone, some charity alone, and some good works alone, when yet the one thing without the second, and the one and the second without the third, is nothing."

But then I asked, "Isn't it possible for a person to have charity and faith and still not do good works? Can't someone love and think about something, but not work on it?" The angelic spirit

All the angels are not only with the Lord, but are also in the Lord; or, what amounts to the same, the Lord is with them and in them.

Arcana Coelestia 363

said to me, "No they can't, except in an ideal, unreal way. They would have to continue in the intention or willingness to do it. Willingness or intention is an act of its own because there is a constant drive towards doing the act, and that will turn into an outer act when some termination occurs. As a result, everyone who is wise views intention and willingness to be a form of inner action, equally as valid as outer action, because God views it that way—provided it actually happens when the opportunity arises."

After that I went down the steps leading out of the Temple of Wisdom and I walked around the grounds. I saw some people sitting under a laurel tree eating figs, so I went over to them and asked if I could have some figs, and they gave me some. And lo and behold, the figs turned into bunches of grapes in my hand. And while I was standing there in amazement the angelic spirit, who was still with me, said, "The figs became bunches of grapes in your hand because figs, due to an inner similarity, symbolize the good qualities produced by charity and its faith on the outer, natural level, while bunches of grapes symbolize the good qualities produced by charity and faith on the inner, spiritual level. It is because of your love for spiritual things that this happened to you. In our world, symbolism shapes everything that happens, everything that comes into being, and all the changes that occur."

Then a desire came over me to know how people can do something good from God and yet do it as if they did it all on their own. So I asked the fig-eaters what they take that to mean. They said, "We can only think that God works it out inwardly in us and through us, and we know nothing about it. Because if we were conscious of doing something good and were therefore acting as if on our own, which is the same as acting on our own, we would be doing something evil, not something good. For everything that people produce on their own, they produce with their own ego, and people's egos are born evil. And how can goodness from God be bonded to evil from ourselves and the two go hand in hand into some action? Our egos constantly breathe the idea of reward into anything having to do with salvation. And by so doing they take the Lord's merit away from Him, even though that's the height of injustice and impiety. In a word, if the goodness that the Lord works in us by means of the Holy Spirit were to flow into our willing and doing, that goodness would be totally befouled and also profaned. But God would never permit it. Now people can indeed think that the good things they do are from God, and call them God's goodness in themselves as if that goodness were their own, but we still don't know what to make of that."

Then I opened my mind and said, "You don't know what to make of it because you are thinking on the basis of the way things appear, and thought established on that basis is false. Your false perspective comes from your belief that all of our willing and thinking and doing and talking are in us, and therefore originate in us. But really there is nothing in us but a condition of being receptive to what flows in. We are not life itself: we are organs that receive life. Only the Lord is life itself, as He says in the gospel according to John: 'Just as the Father has *life in Himself,* so He has given the *Son to have life in Himself* ' (John 5.26; cf. 11.25, 14.6,19). Two things constitute life: love and wisdom or, what is the same thing, love's goodness and wisdom's truth. These two flow in from God and are received by us. We feel them as if they were in us. And because we feel them as if they were in us, they

Heaven and hell are from the human race.

HEAVEN AND HELL 311

also go out to others as if from us. The Lord has gifted us with that feeling in order for us to be affected by what flows in and receive it and have it stay with us. But everything evil also flows in from outside us—not from God but from hell—and from the start we receive it with delight because we were born that way. Therefore, the amount of goodness we receive from God can only equal the amount of evil we have removed from ourselves as if by our own power, which is done by both working on ourselves and putting our faith in the Lord.

"An analogy will show how love and wisdom, and charity and faith, or speaking more generally, goodness coming from love and charity and truth coming from wisdom and faith, flow in; and how what flows in appears from our point of view to be in us and to come from us. With sight, hearing, smell, taste, and touch, everything we perceive with the organs of these senses flows in from outside of us but is sensed in those organs. It is the same with the organs of our inner senses, with the sole difference that into the latter flow spiritual things beyond our perception, while into the former flow natural things within our perception. So we are organs that receive life from God. As a result, as much as we stop doing what is evil, we become that receptive to what is good. The Lord gives each one of us the power to stop doing evil because He gives us the power to will and understand as if we did it ourselves. And whatever action we take using the will and the intellect that seem to be our own, or to put it another way, using the freedom of our will and the reasoning of our intellect, that action becomes a permanent part of us. This is the Lord's method for bringing us into a state where we are bonded with Him; and this is the condition in which the Lord reforms, regenerates and saves us. The life that flows into us is a vitality coming from the Lord. It is also called the spirit of God. The Word terms it the Holy Spirit, which is said to enlighten us, to bring us to life, and even to function in us. This vitality, however, is shaped and individualized by the structure our particular loves and insights impose on each one of us.

"You are also capable of knowing that all the goodness of love and charity and all the truth from wisdom and faith flow in and do not exist in us, if you consider this: thinking we are born with that goodness and truth leads inexorably to thinking that God poured Himself into us and therefore we are partially gods. But people whose beliefs lead them to think such thoughts become devils and stink like cadavers. For another thing, what are our actions other than our mind doing something? For whatever our mind wills and thinks about, we use the instrument of our body to do. Therefore, when the Lord leads our mind, He also leads our actions. And the Lord leads our mind and actions when we believe in Him. If this wasn't true, then tell me if you can why the Lord would order us a thousand times in a thousand passages to love our neighbor, to do the good deeds of charity and produce its fruits like a tree, and to do what He commands; and do it all in order to be saved. And why else did He say that we will be judged by our works or deeds, those of us doing good ones being judged to heaven and life, and those of us doing evil ones to hell and death? How could the Lord say such things if everything coming from us was done for merit and was therefore evil? You ought to know, then, that if the mind is a form of charity, the actions too

Angels know no greater happiness than caring for and instructing those who arrive from the world.

ARCANA COELESTIA 454

Angels are in the most

complete human form

and enjoy every sense.

HEAVEN AND HELL 170

will be forms of charity. But if the mind is a form of faith alone, or faith separate from spiritual charity, the actions too will be forms of that faith; and that faith is merit-seeking because its charity is natural, not spiritual. Charity's faith is different, because charity does not want to take merit, and as a result, neither does its faith."

After they had heard all this, the ones sitting under the laurel tree said, "We understand that what you said is right, but we still don't understand it." To this I replied, "Your understanding that what I said is right comes from the general perception that light inflowing from heaven gives to us when we hear something true. But your lack of understanding is due to your own perception, which is something we all have from light inflowing from the world. These two perceptions, one internal and the other external, one spiritual and the other natural, combine to make one perception in those who are wise. You too can combine the two into one if you look to the Lord and remove what is evil in yourselves."

Because they understood these points as well, I took some branches from the laurel tree under which we sat, handed them to them and asked, "Do you believe these are from me or from the Lord?" They said they came through me as if they were from me. And lo and behold, the branches blossomed in their hands.

But as I left there I saw a cedar table; and on it, under an olive tree that was showing new growth and that had a vine coiled around its trunk, there was a book. I looked right at it, and to my surprise it was a book written through me called *Angelic Wisdom on Divine Love and Divine Wisdom* and also *on Divine Providence*. And I told them that that book fully demonstrated that we are organs that receive life; we are not life.

Afterwards I went home from that garden exhilarated, and the angelic spirit went with me. He said to me on the way, "Do you want to see a clear example of what faith and charity are, and so what faith is when separated from charity and what it is when connected to charity? I will make it visible to you if you like." So I answered, "Go ahead." He said, "Instead of faith and charity, think of light and heat and you will see it clearly. For faith at its core is truth that comes from wisdom, and charity at its core is a feeling that comes from love. In heaven truth coming from wisdom is light and the feeling of love is heat. The light and heat in the angels' world are nothing else. This analogy will allow you to see clearly what faith separate from charity is, as opposed to faith connected with charity. Faith separate from charity is like the light in winter, while faith connected with charity is like the light in spring. The light in winter, which is a light separate from heat because it is connected with cold, strips the trees of their leaves, hardens the earth, kills off the grasses, and also freezes all forms of water. But spring light, which is a light connected with heat, energizes trees to produce first leaves, then flowers, and finally fruit; it opens up and softens the earth so that it produces grasses, groundcover, flowers, and bushes, and also melts the ice so that water flows again from the springs. It is utterly the same with faith and charity. Faith separate from charity kills everything; faith connected with charity brings all things to life. In our spiritual world this bringing to life and that killing off can be seen in a living way, since here faith is light and charity is heat. For where faith has been connected with charity, there you'll find paradisal gardens, flowerbeds, and greenery at their most pleasant according to how connected the faith and charity are. But where faith has been separated from charity, there you won't even find grass; and where it is green, it is from thorn bushes, brambles, and nettles. The heat and light coming from the Lord as a sun have this effect *in* angels and spirits and therefore also *around* them."

By that point there were some clergymen not far from us. The angelic spirit called them justifiers and sanctifiers of people by faith alone. He also called them specialists in mystery. We made these same points to them, and we demonstrated them until they could see that it was true. And when we asked, "Isn't that so?" they turned their backs and said, "We didn't hear what you said." So we shouted at them and said, "Then listen again!" But they put both hands over their ears and yelled, "We don't *want* to hear it."

From *Apocalypse Revealed* 875

Epilogue

I foresee that many who read the narratives . . . will believe them to be inventions of the imagination. But I affirm in
truth that they are not inventions, but were truly seen and heard;
not seen and heard in any sleeping state of mind, but in a state of
full wakefulness. For it has pleased the Lord to . . . open the interiors of my mind or spirit, whereby I have been permitted to be
in the spiritual world with angels, and at the same time in the
natural world with people, and this now [has happened for]
twenty-seven years.

Emanuel Swedenborg
True Christian Religion 851

Further Reading

Those interested in consulting the full text of Swedenborg's writings on angels should read the following works, all available from the Swedenborg Foundation:

Apocalypse Revealed
First published in 1766, this work is a complete verse-by-verse exposition of the symbolic meaning of the biblical book of Revelation, treating of the Christian church, the last judgment in the spiritual world, and the New Church, which Swedenborg called the New Jerusalem. Many of Swedenborg's visionary experiences in the spiritual world can be found in this two-volume work.

Arcana Coelestia
This twelve-volume work was first published from 1749 through 1756. This work is a detailed exposition of the symbolic meaning of the biblical books of Genesis and Exodus. Important Swedenborgian doctrines, such as the law of correspondences, are discussed and explained in the various volumes; and passages from the Word are cited in confirmation. Interchapter material contains extensive descriptions of life in the spiritual world, as well as doctrinal matters.

Conjugial Love
First published in 1768, this definitive work on love and marriage explains the origin and essentially sacred character of love between a man and a woman in marriage as related to the marriage of good and truth

in the Lord—the union of divine love and divine wisdom. It also discusses the eternal quality of the marital state and the nature of human sexuality. It contains reports of many conversations with angels. This work is also available in recent translations by David Gladish, titled *Love in Marriage,* and by N. Bruce Rogers, titled *Married Love.*

Heaven and Hell

First published in 1758, this remarkable work is a detailed description of life after death, reported by Swedenborg from his actual visionary journeys to heaven and hell. Our entrance into the spiritual world, the nature of the world of spirits, and the place of preparation for our eternal dwelling place are explained. The structure and life of heaven and hell, uses of angelic societies, the marriage of angelic spirits, children in heaven, angelic language, and many other topics are discussed in this famous work.

Five Memorable Relations

Written in 1766 but first published after Swedenborg's death, this work is a brief account of Swedenborg's experiences in the spiritual world. It is available only in vol. 2 of *Posthumous Theological Works.*

The True Christian Religion

Published in 1771, the final treatise published by Swedenborg in his lifetime, this two-volume work contains "the universal theology of the New Church" and fully propounds New Church doctrine. Among the topics that individual chapters address are God the Creator, the Lord as redeemer, the Holy Spirit, Sacred Scripture, faith, charity, free will, and repentance. Swedenborg illustrates these subjects through his "memorable experiences" in the spiritual world.

About the Contributors

Leonard Fox studied at New York, Columbia, London, and Munich Universities; and has taught Sanskrit, Russian, and linguistics at various universities. He has published books on Albanian customary law and Albanian grammar, and on Malagasy poetry. Mr. Fox is the editor of *Arcana: Inner Dimensions of Spirituality,* a journal devoted to studies in comparative religion and the theology of Emanuel Swedenborg.

Donald L. Rose is a Swedenborgian minister who was educated at the Academy of the New Church in Bryn Athyn, Pennsylvania, and at the University of Grenoble in France. He has served his ministry in Australia, New Zealand, France, and Holland. During nine years in London, he participated in the work of the Swedenborg Society. He has produced a number of Swedenborg studies designed for young people, including a study entitled *The Human Face.* Rev. Rose currently edits the monthly *New Church Life* and serves on the board of directors of the Swedenborg Foundation.

David Gladish was a scholar, writer, and translator who had a lifelong interest in the works of Emanuel Swedenborg. Dr. Gladish taught rhetoric and literature for seven years at the

University of Illinois, where he also received his Ph.D.; and then taught for eleven years at Franklin College. In addition to being a prolific essayist and poet, Dr. Gladish also edited Sir William Davenant's *Gondibert*. Among his other translations of Swedenborg's writings are *Seeing's Believing* (a translation of *The Doctrine of Faith)* and *Love in Marriage* (a translation of *Conjugial Love).*

Jonathan Rose received a B.A. and an M.Div. in religion from the Academy of the New Church in Bryn Athyn, Pennsylvania; he also holds an M.A. and Ph.D. in Latin from Bryn Mawr College. Dr. Rose is a Latin translator, curator of the Swedenborgiana Library, and assistant professor of Greek and religion at the Bryn Athyn College of the New Church. He has also written a neo-Latin morphological analysis algorithm for software called NeoSearch; serves as a consultant on a forthcoming Latin/English version of Swedenborg's *Spiritual Experiences*; and is currently translating Swedenborg's *Apocalypse Revealed.*

Martha Gyllenhaal, who contributed the original art, received a B.A. in painting from Carnegie-Mellon University and an M.A. in art history from Temple University. She teaches at Bryn Athyn College of the New Church and is acting head of the Humanities Division there. Ms. Gyllenhaal's paintings are in many private collections, both in this country and abroad, and have been exhibited in a number of galleries.